# Spring

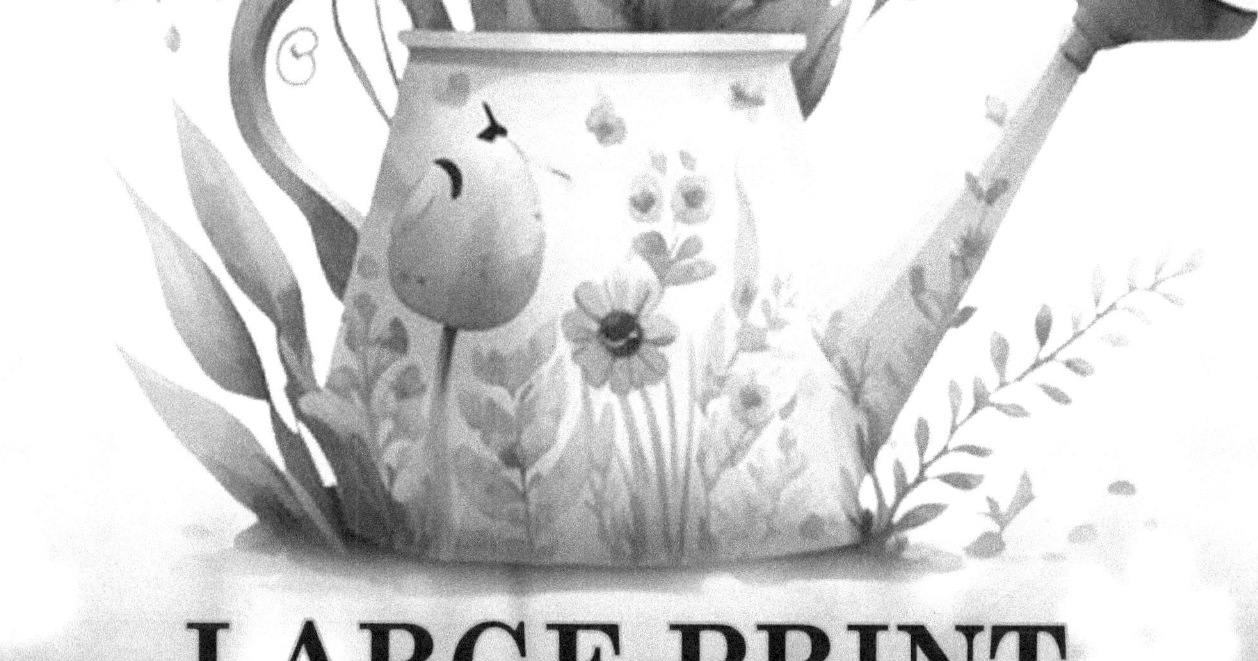

# LARGE PRINT
# ADULT COLORING BOOK

this book belongs to

_______________________

_______________________

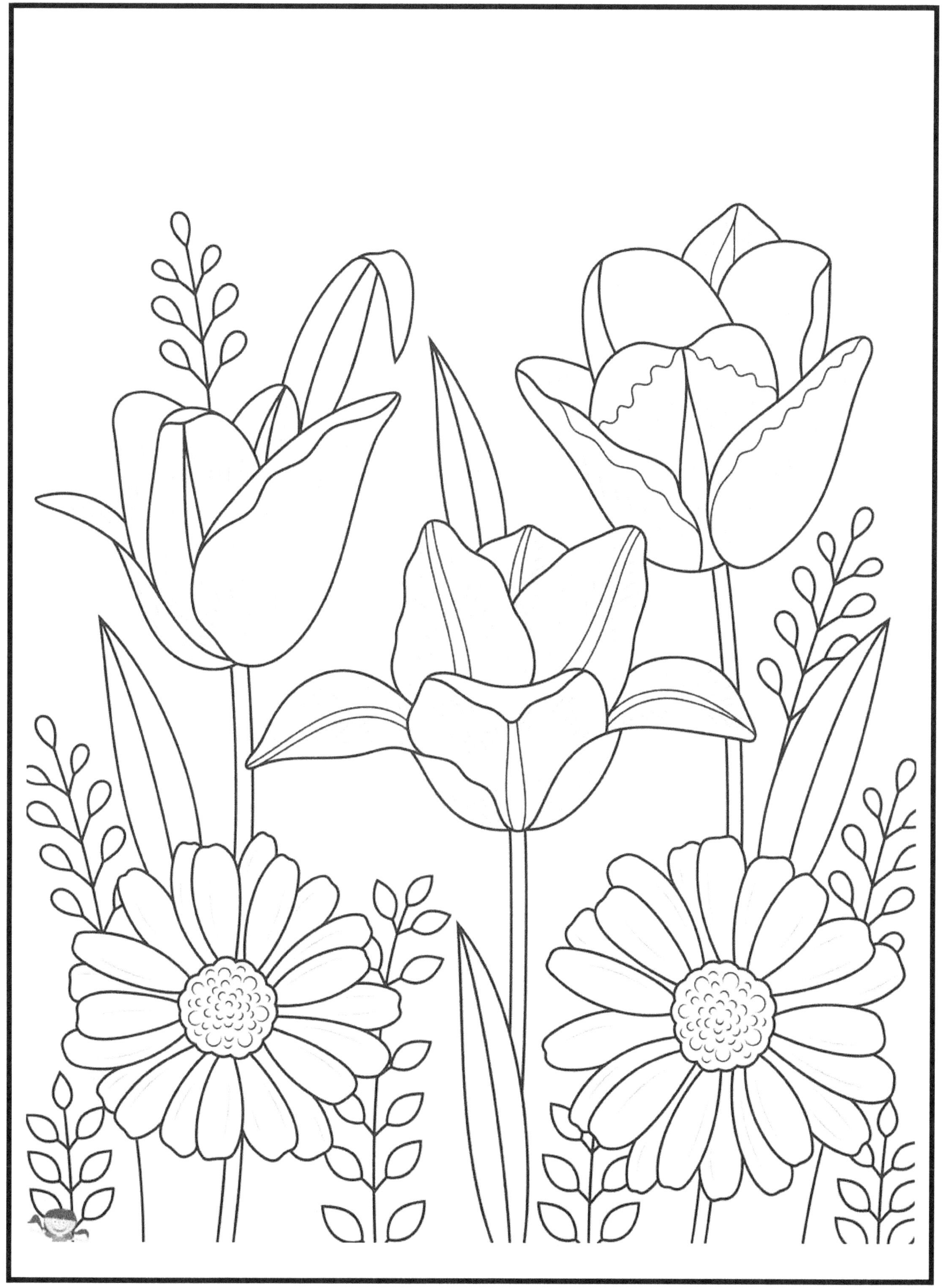

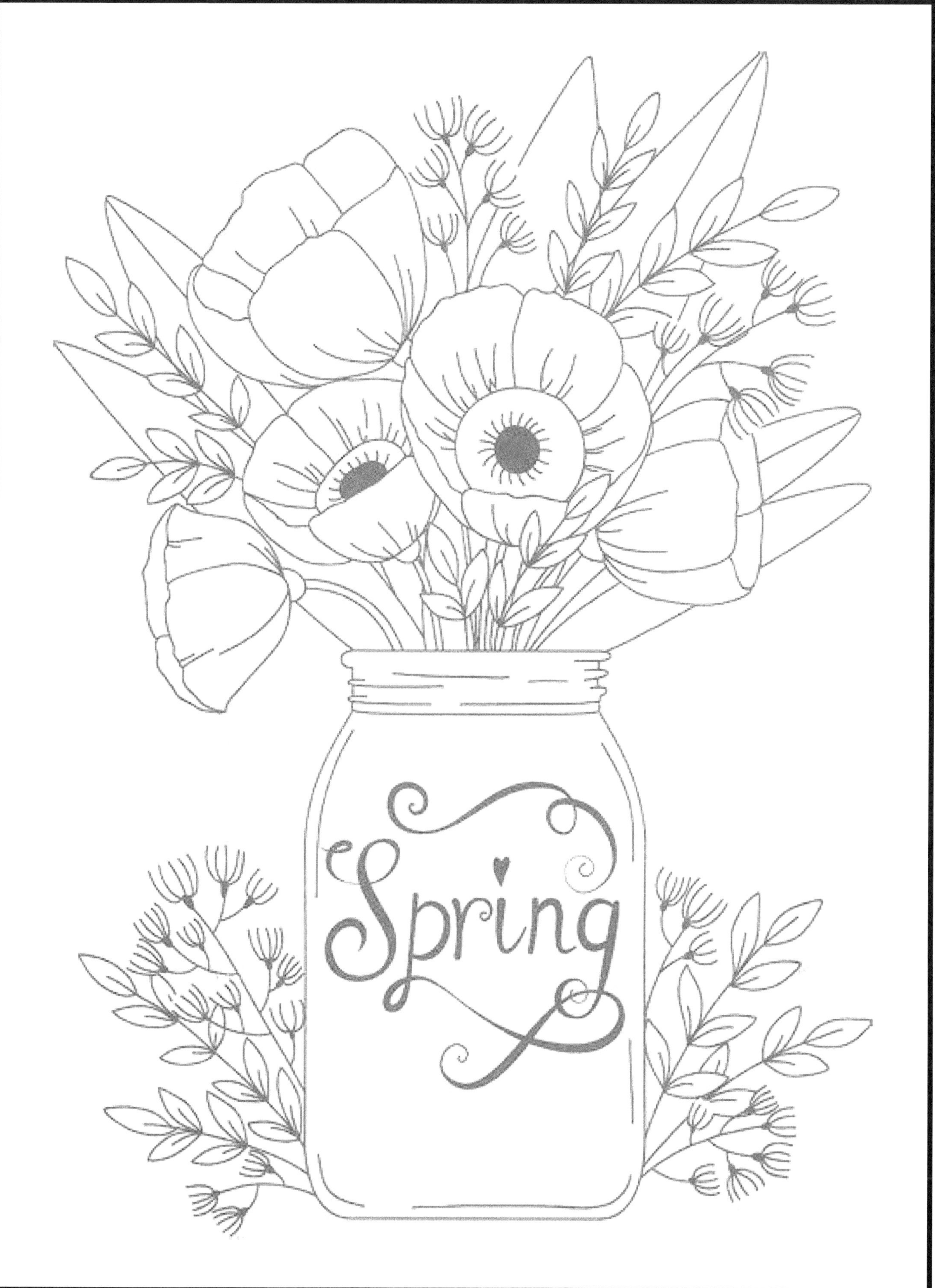

Spring

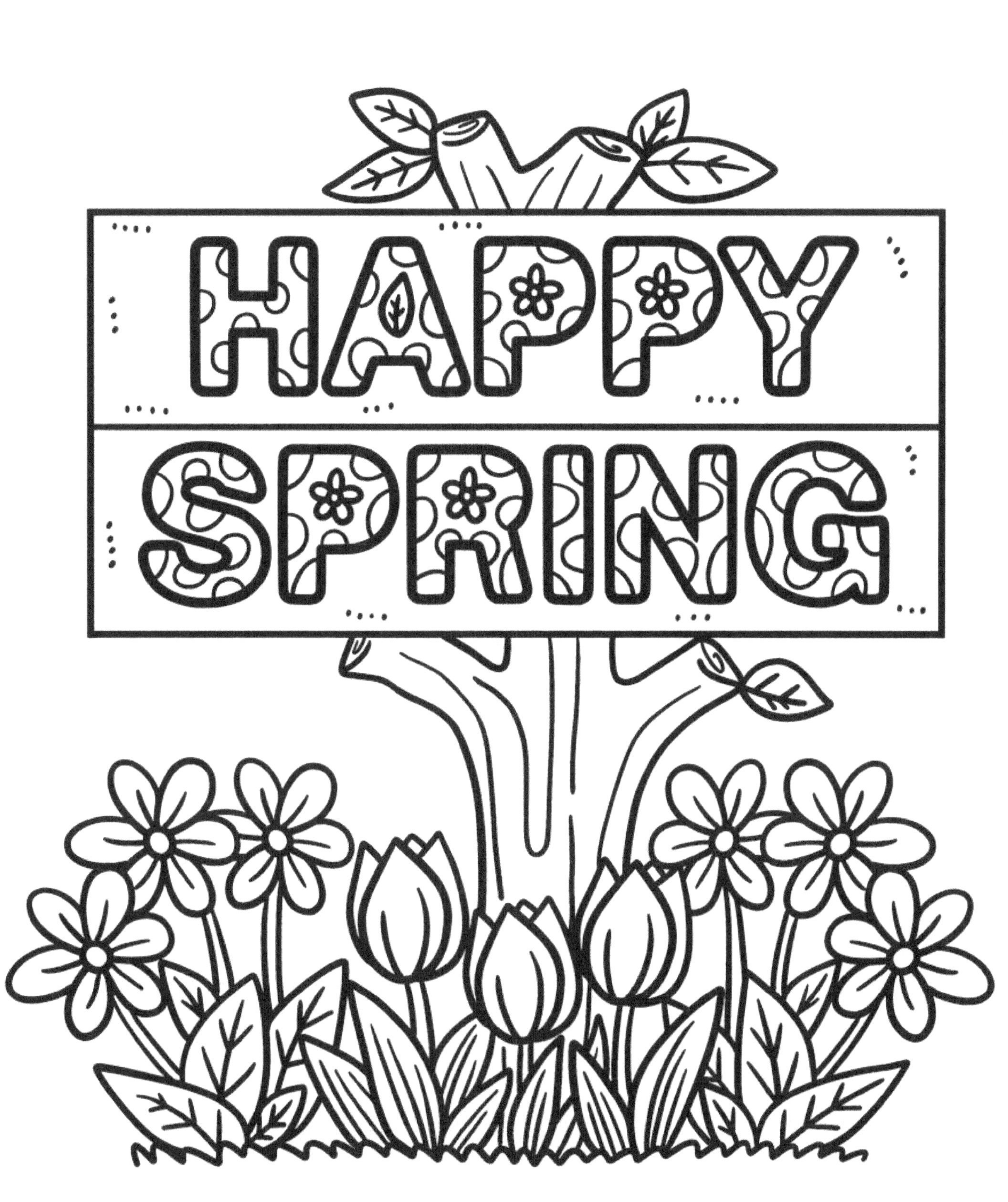

HAPPY
SPRING

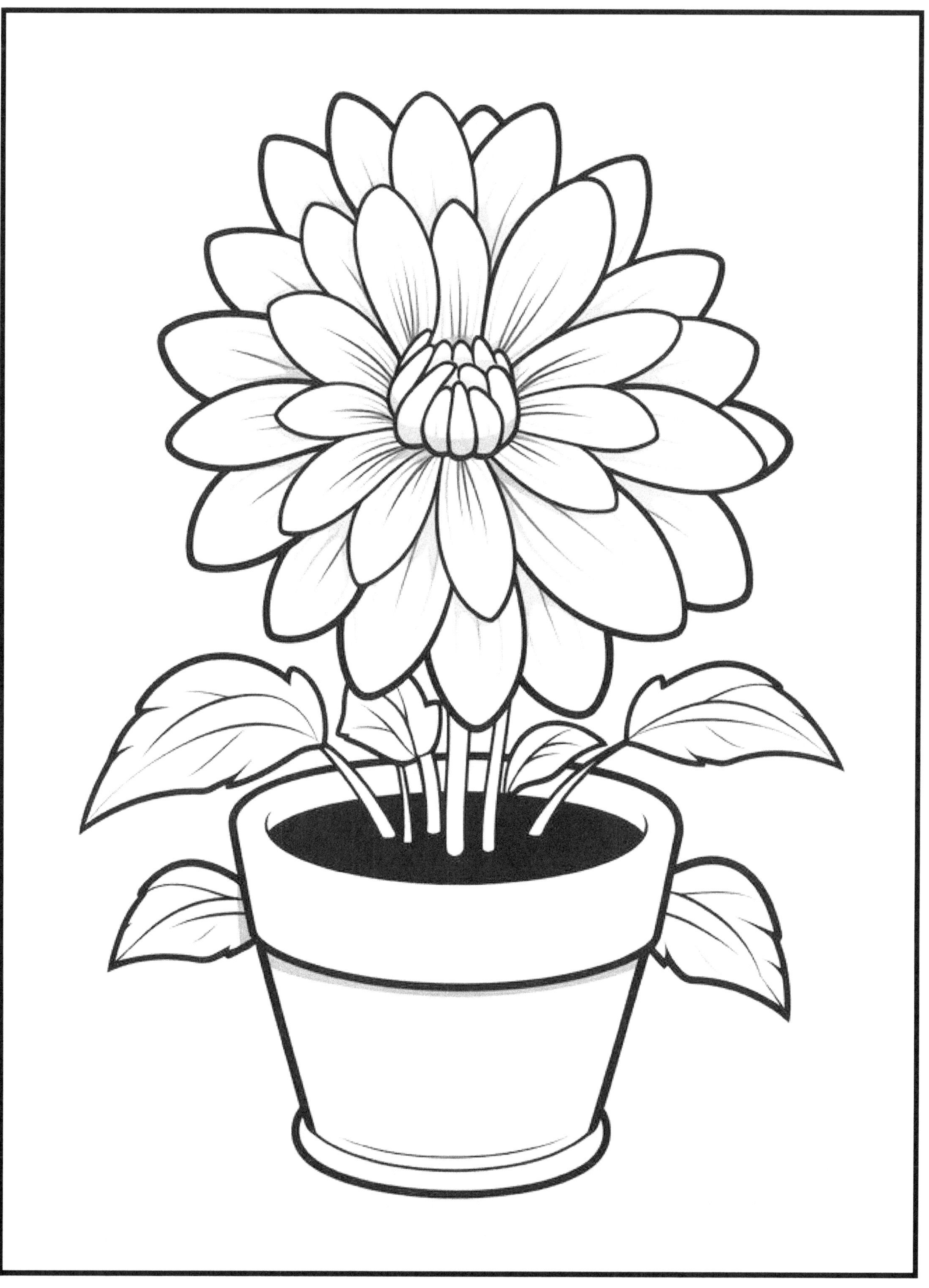

BEST

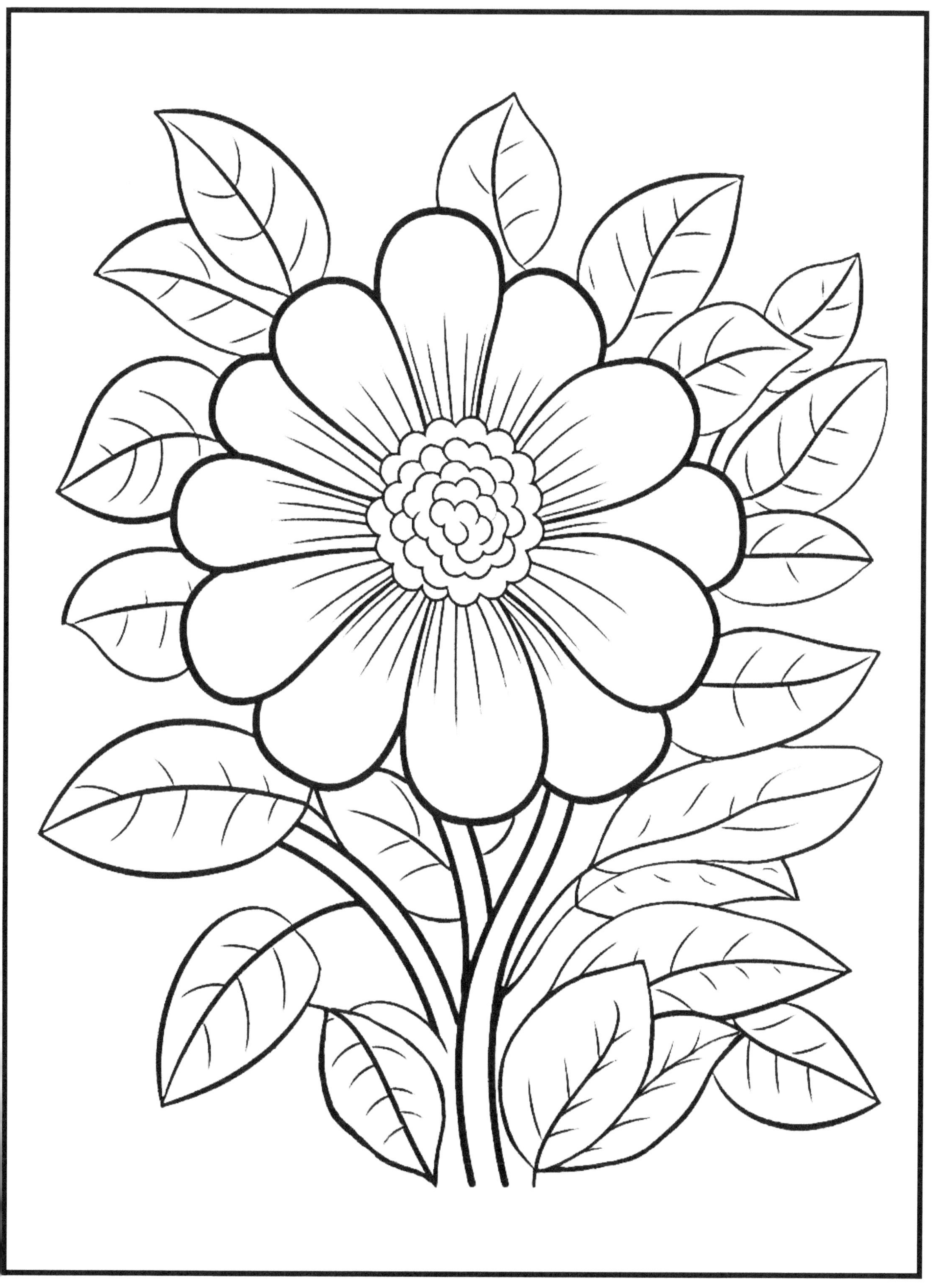

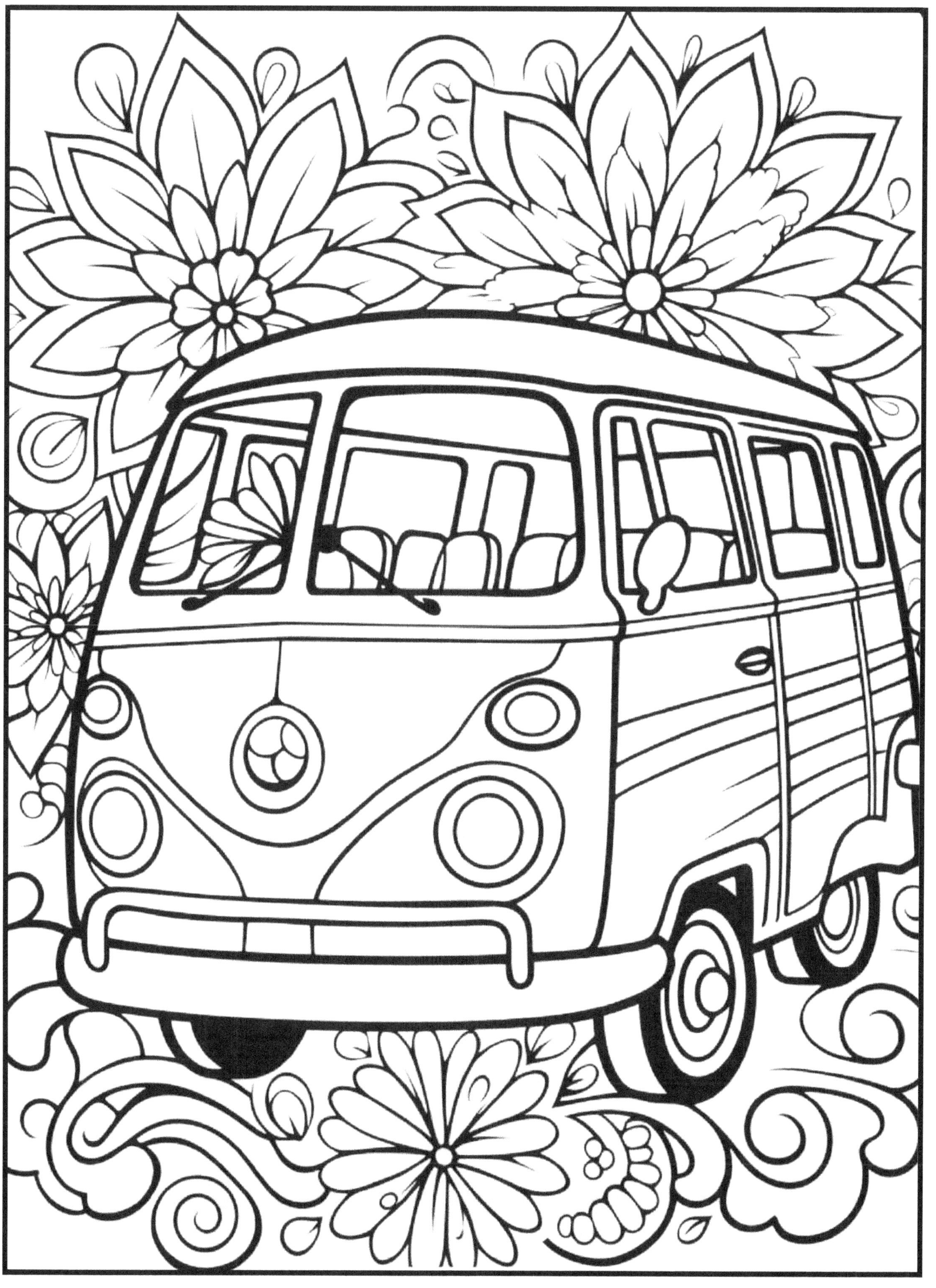

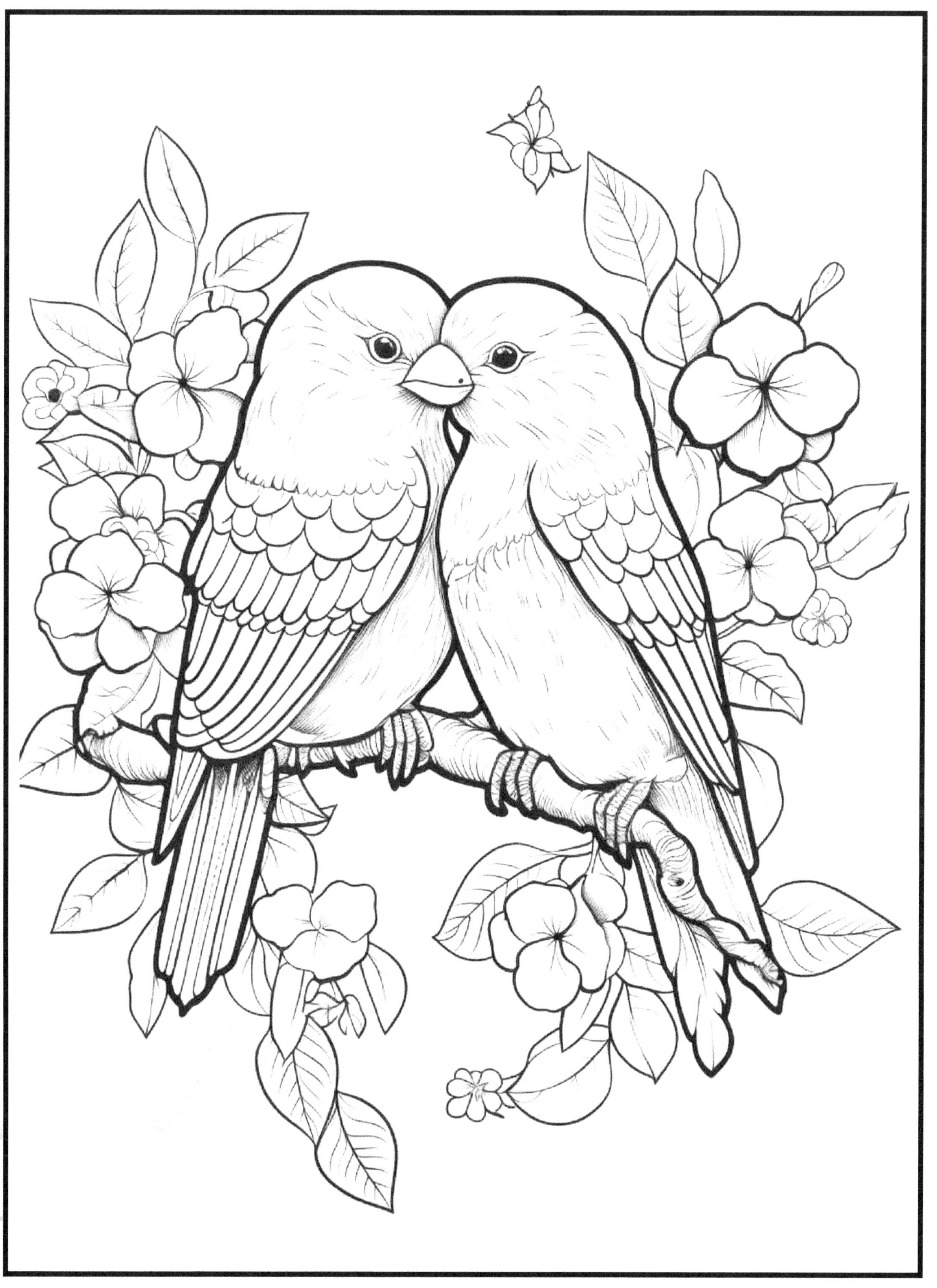

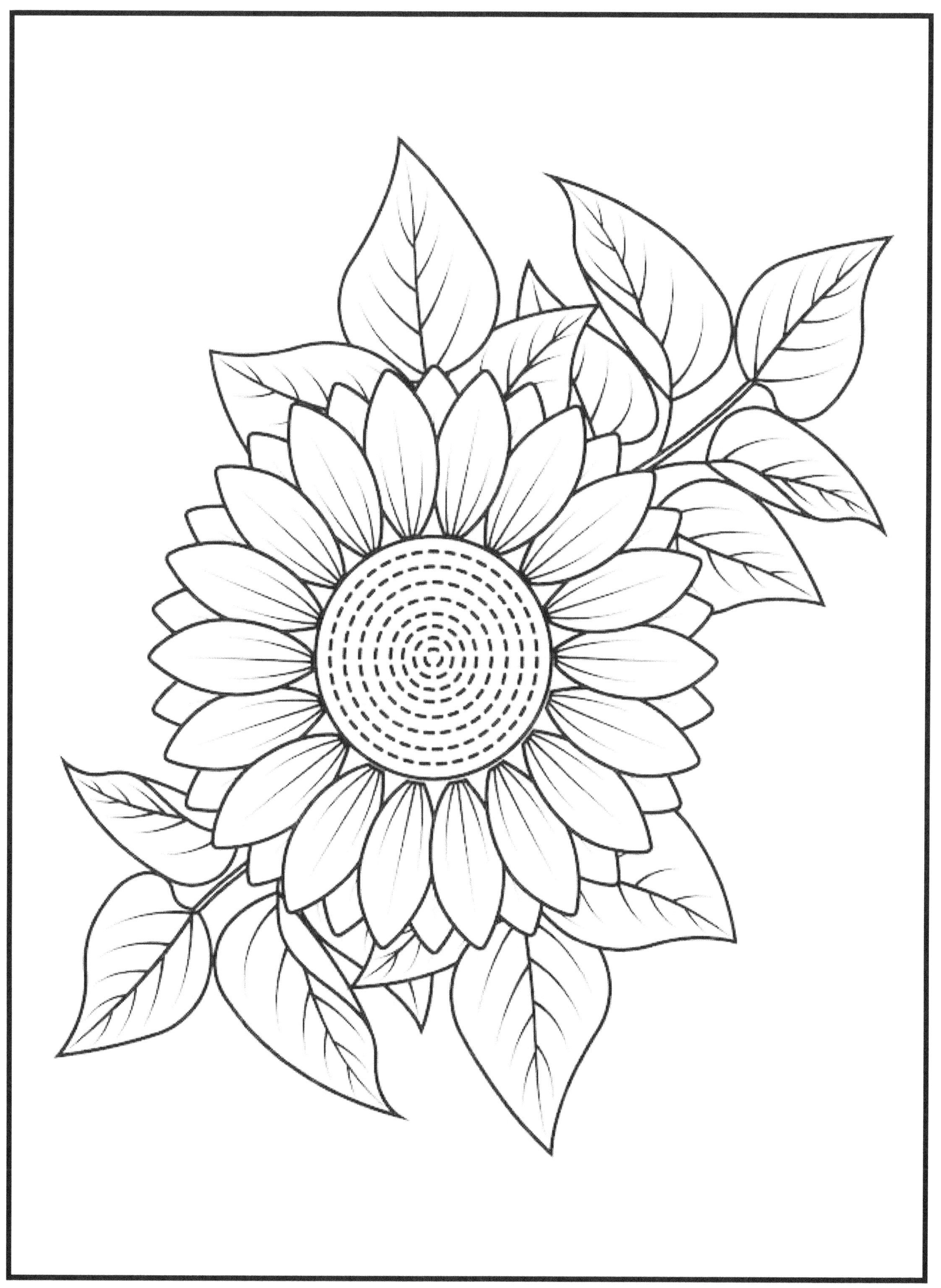

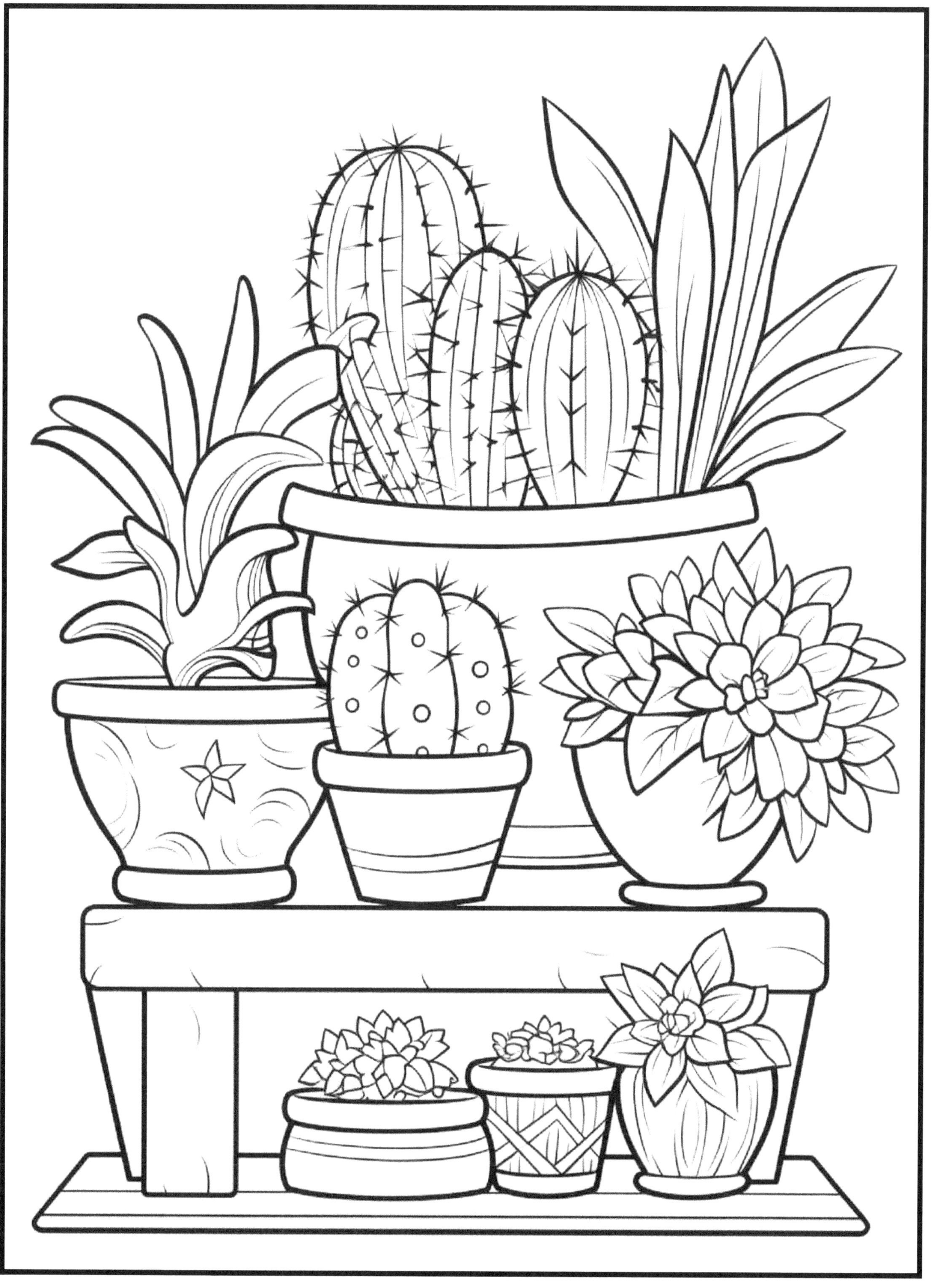

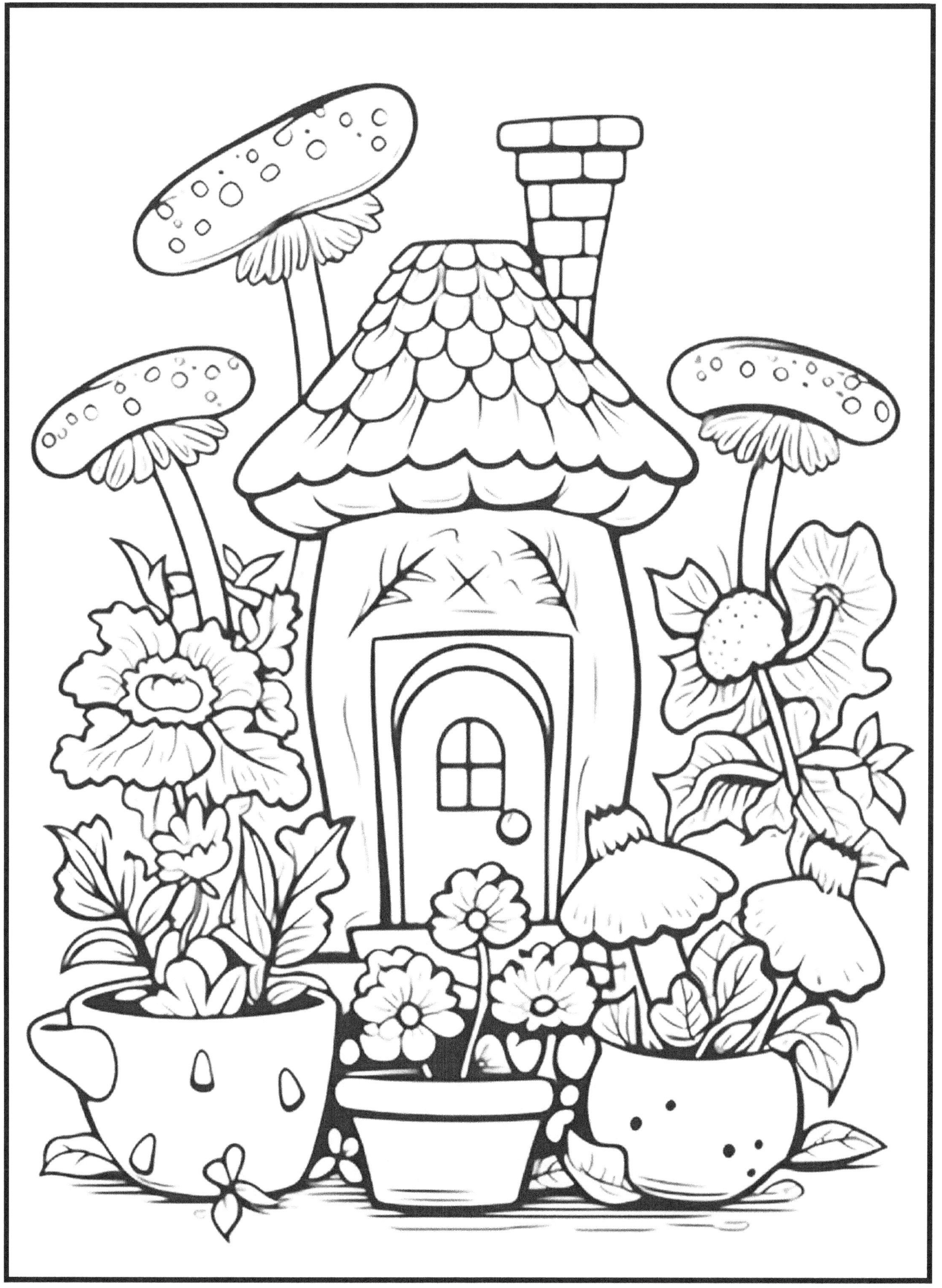

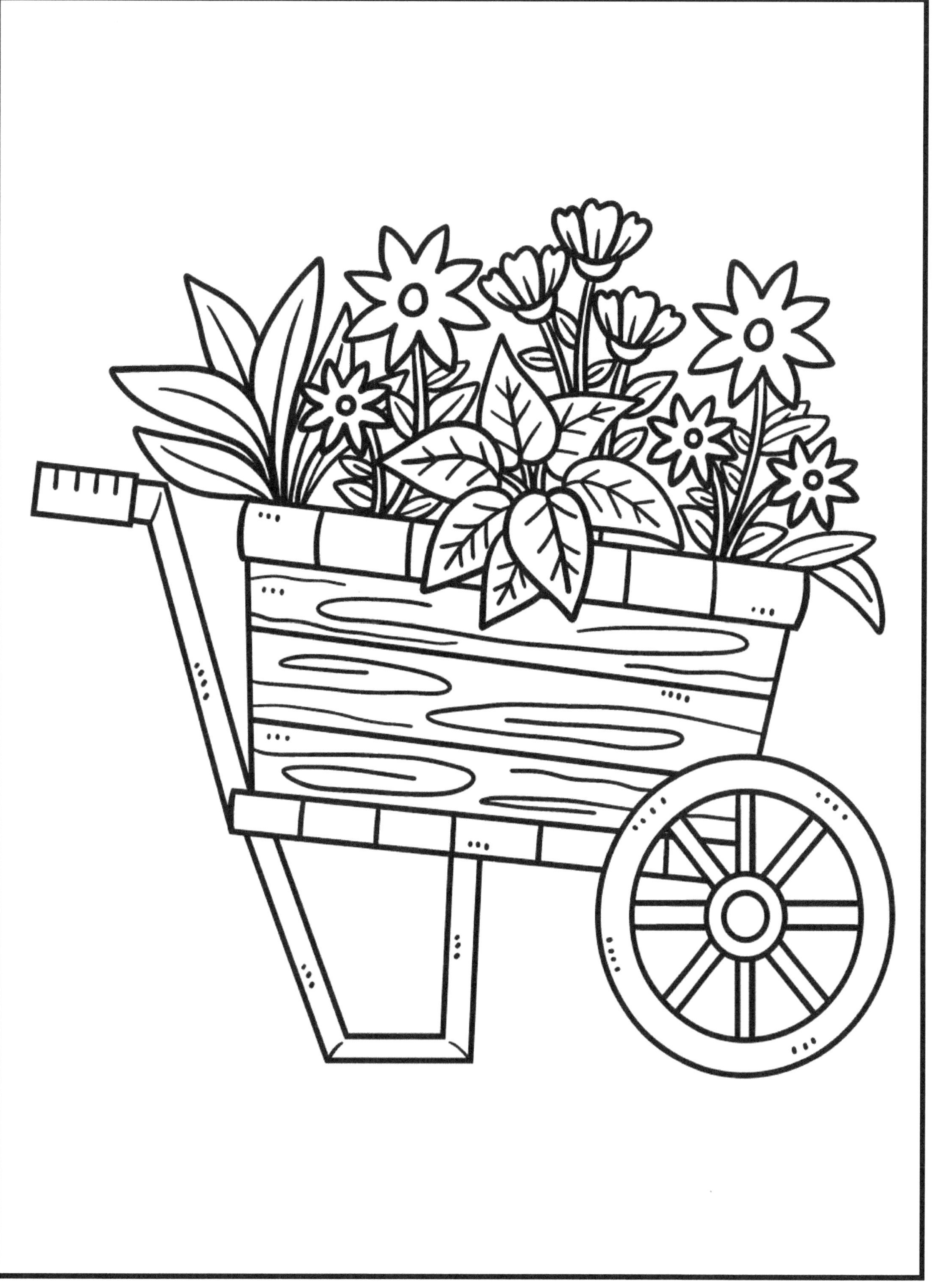

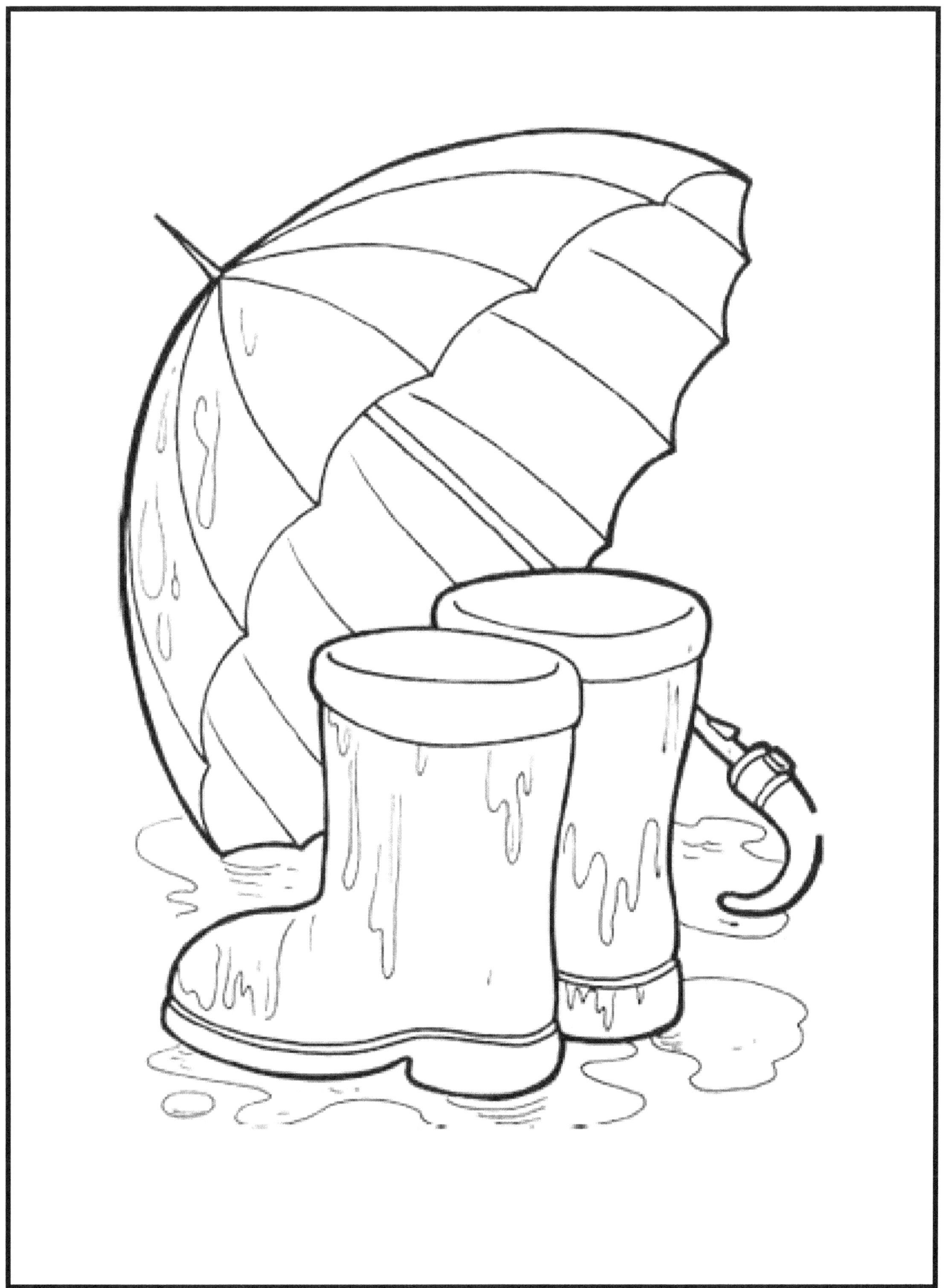

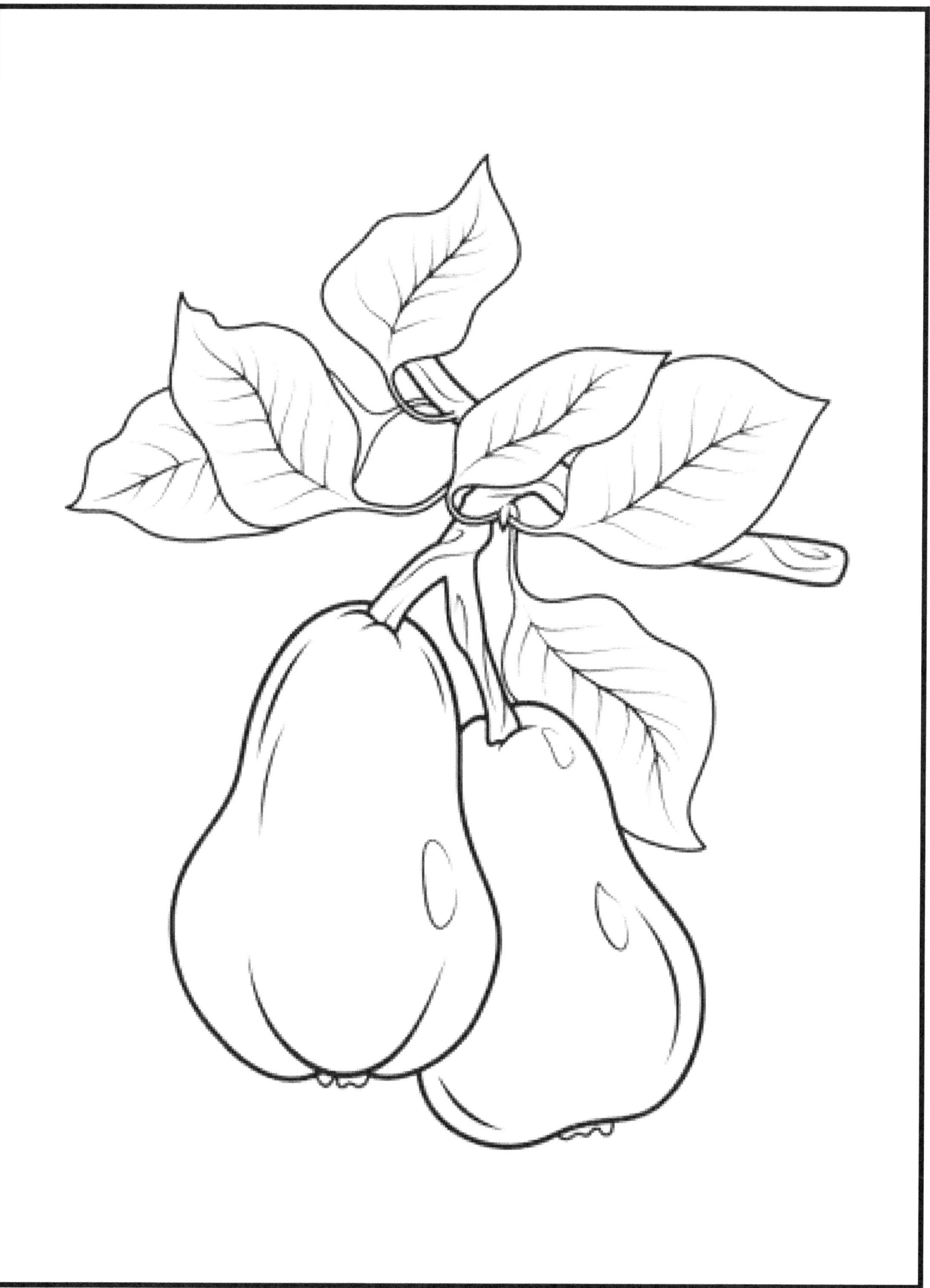

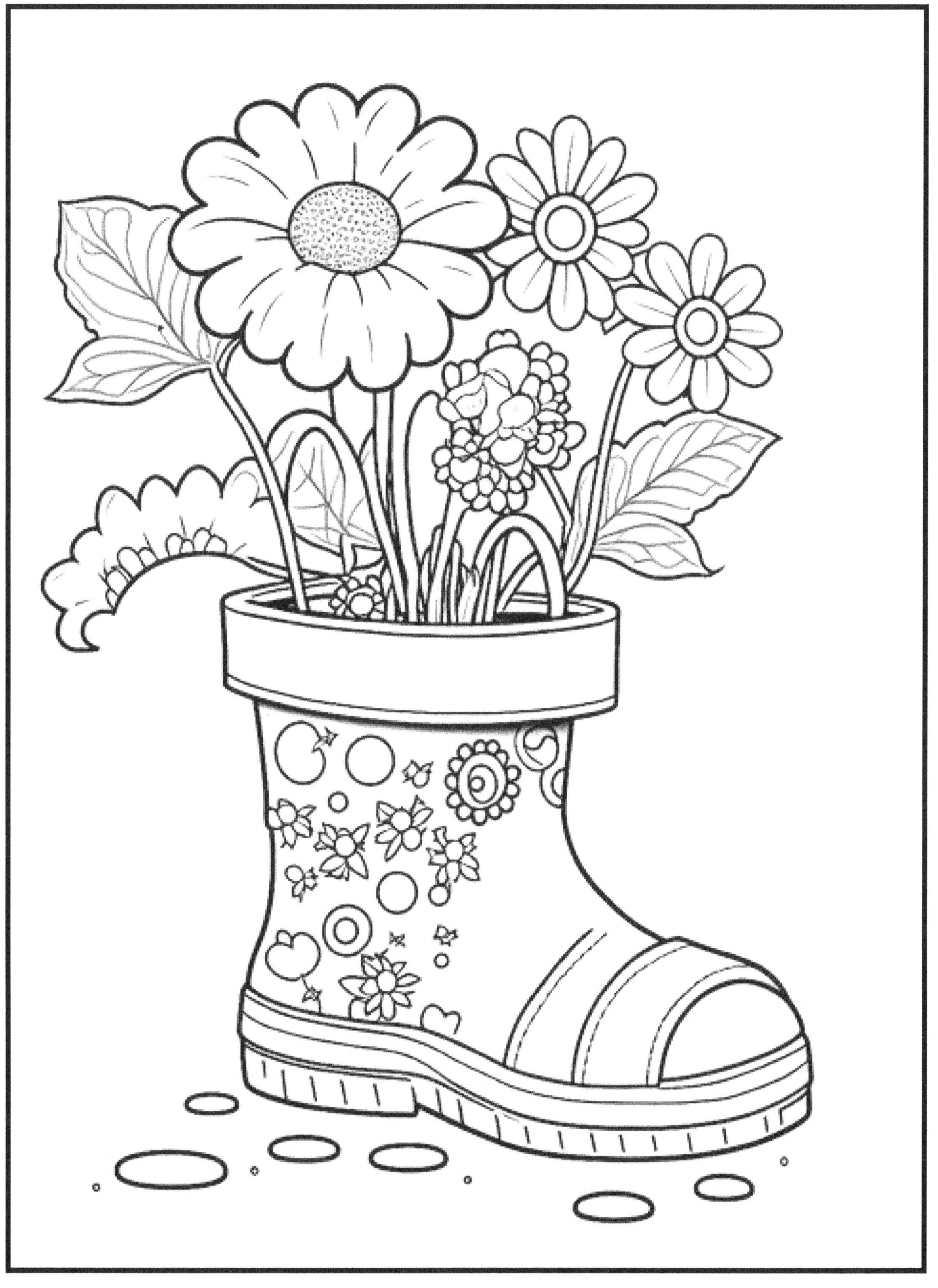

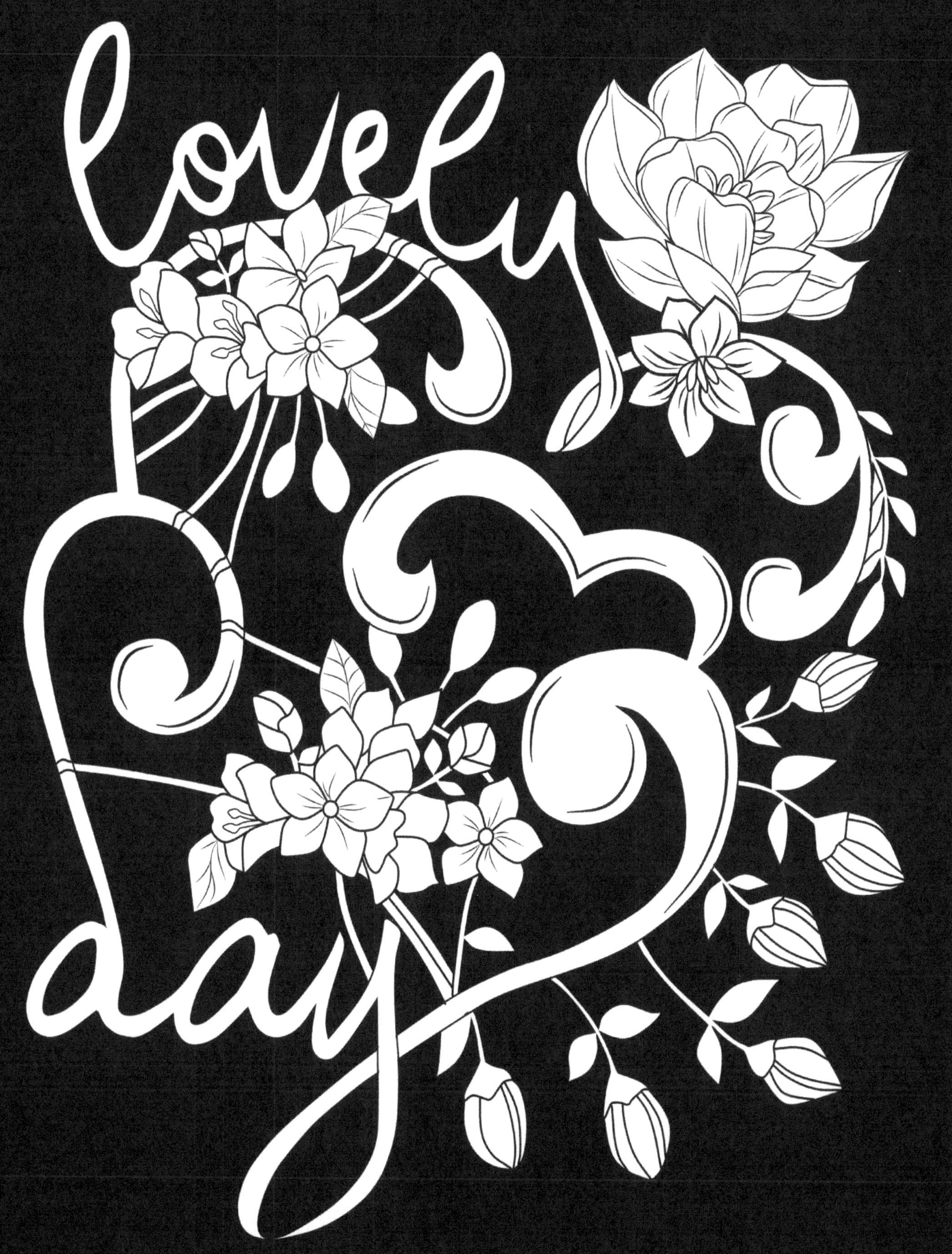

lovely
day

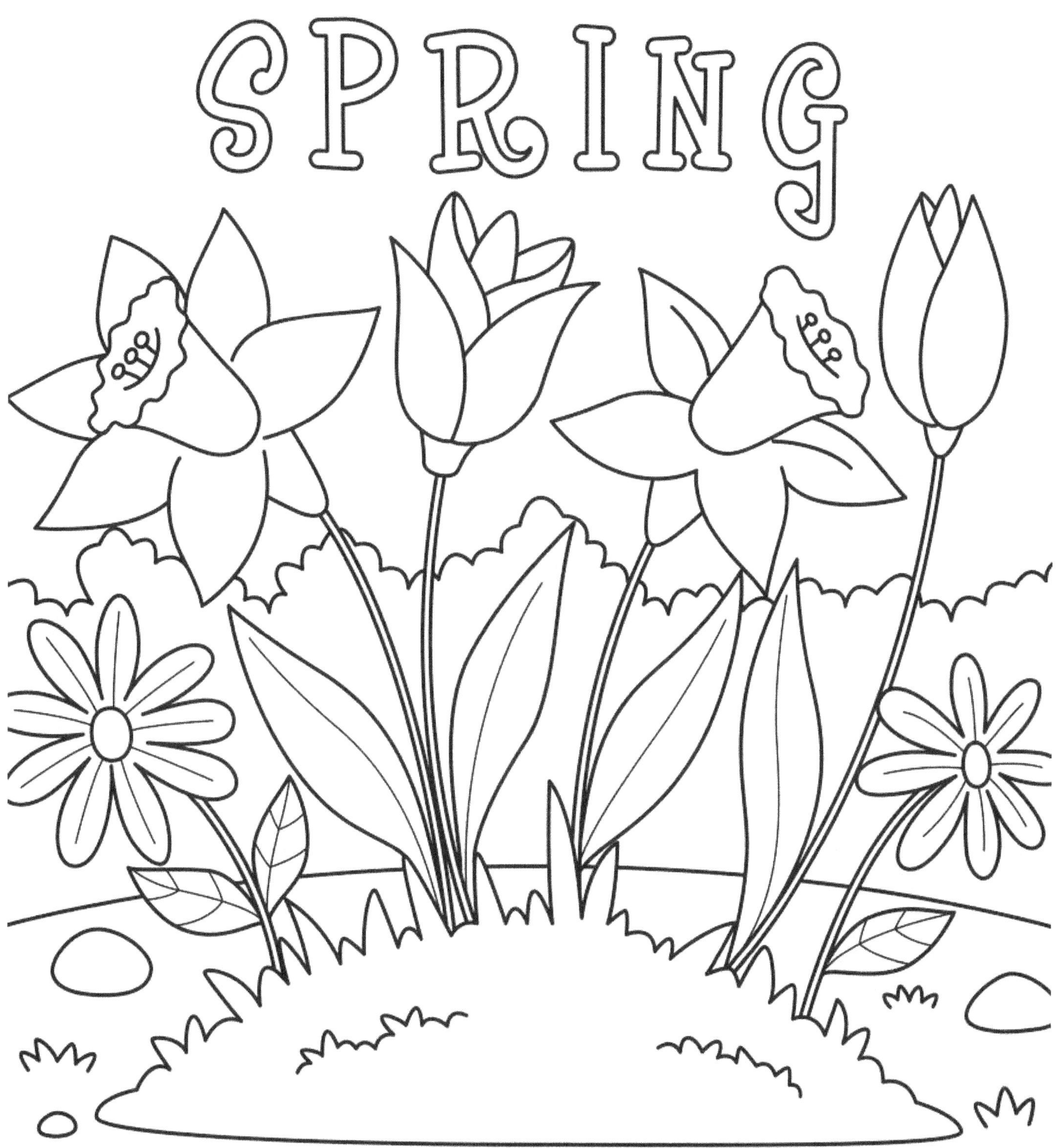

SPRING

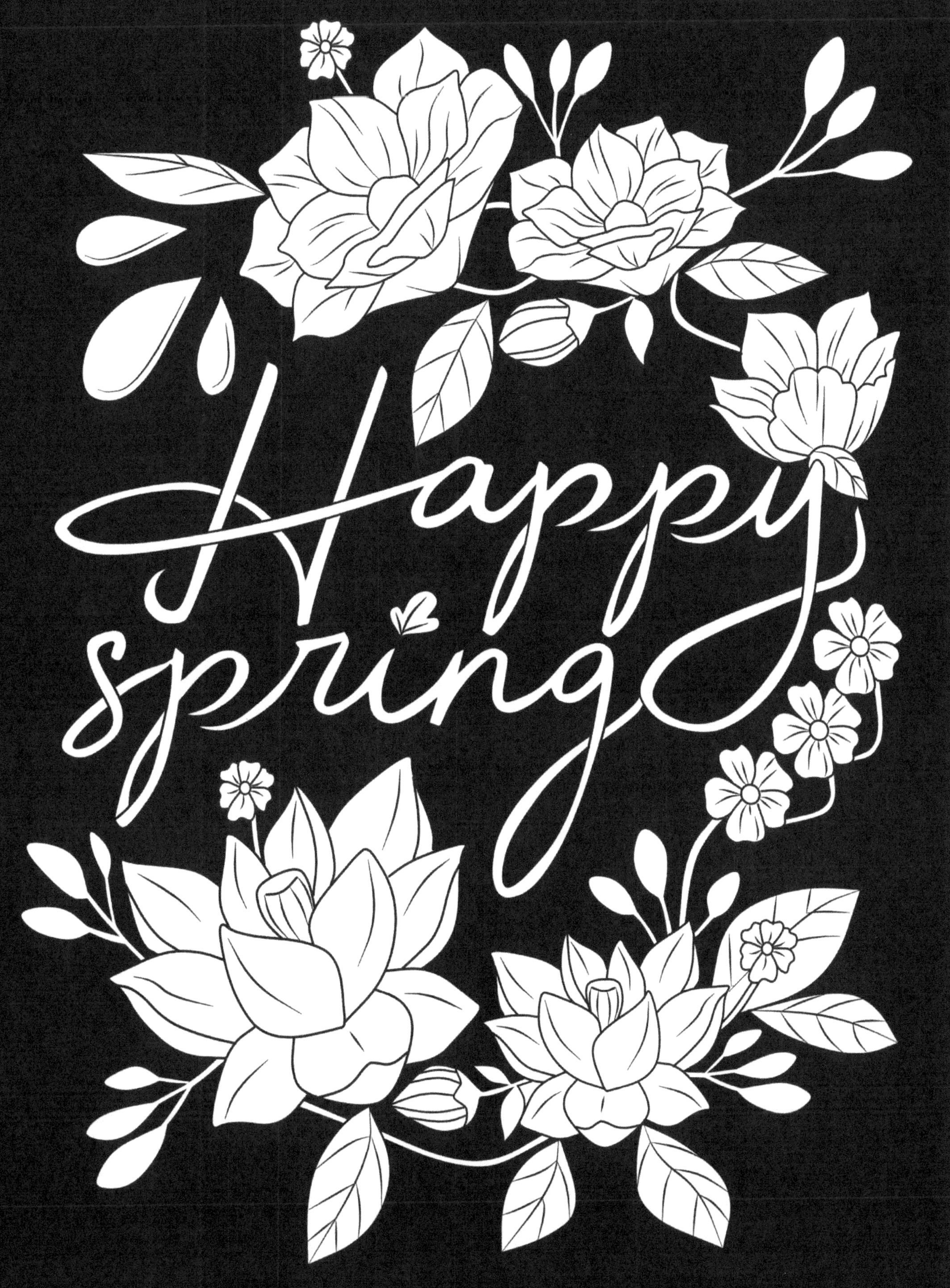

Happy
spring

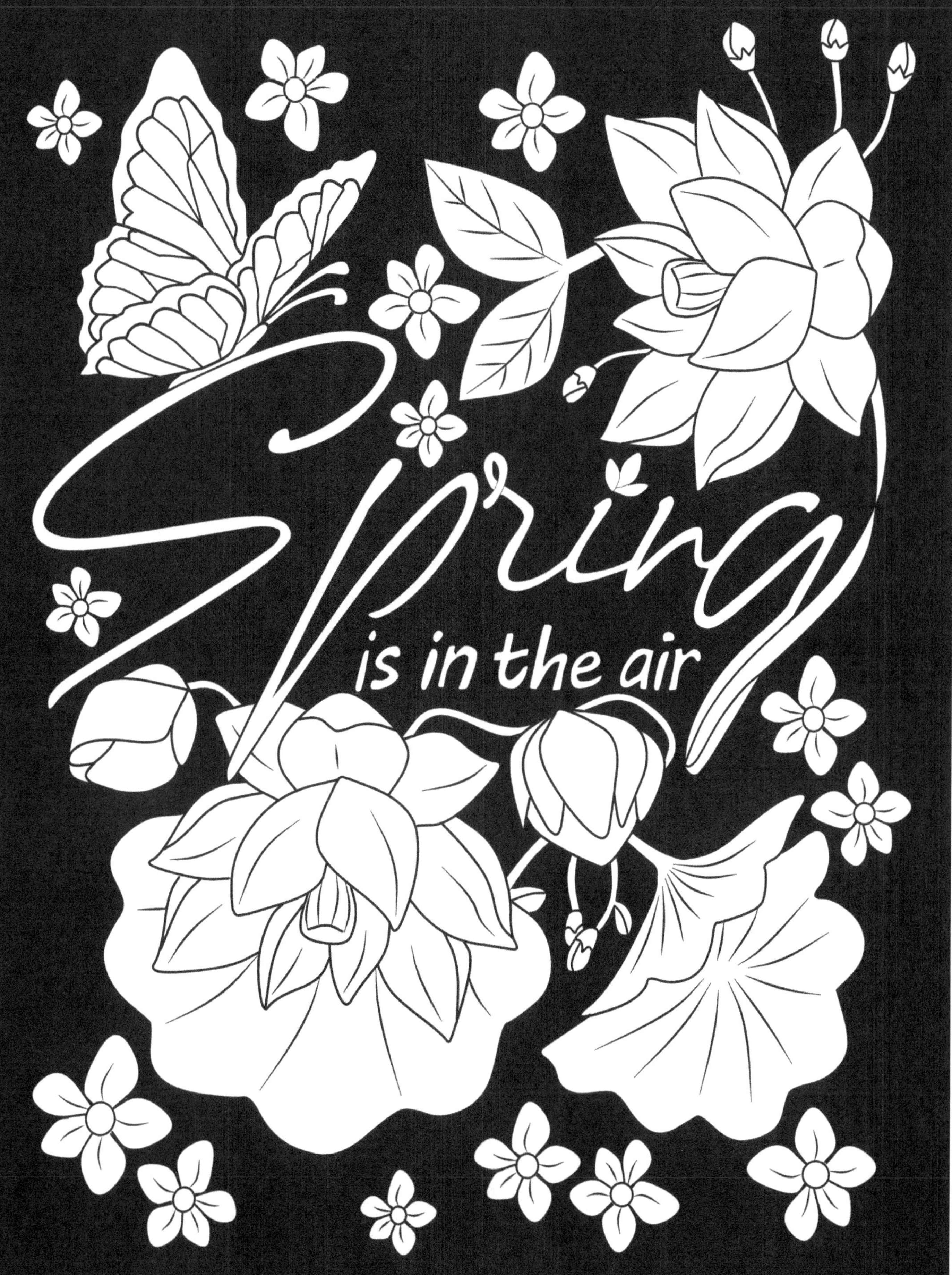

Spring
is in the air

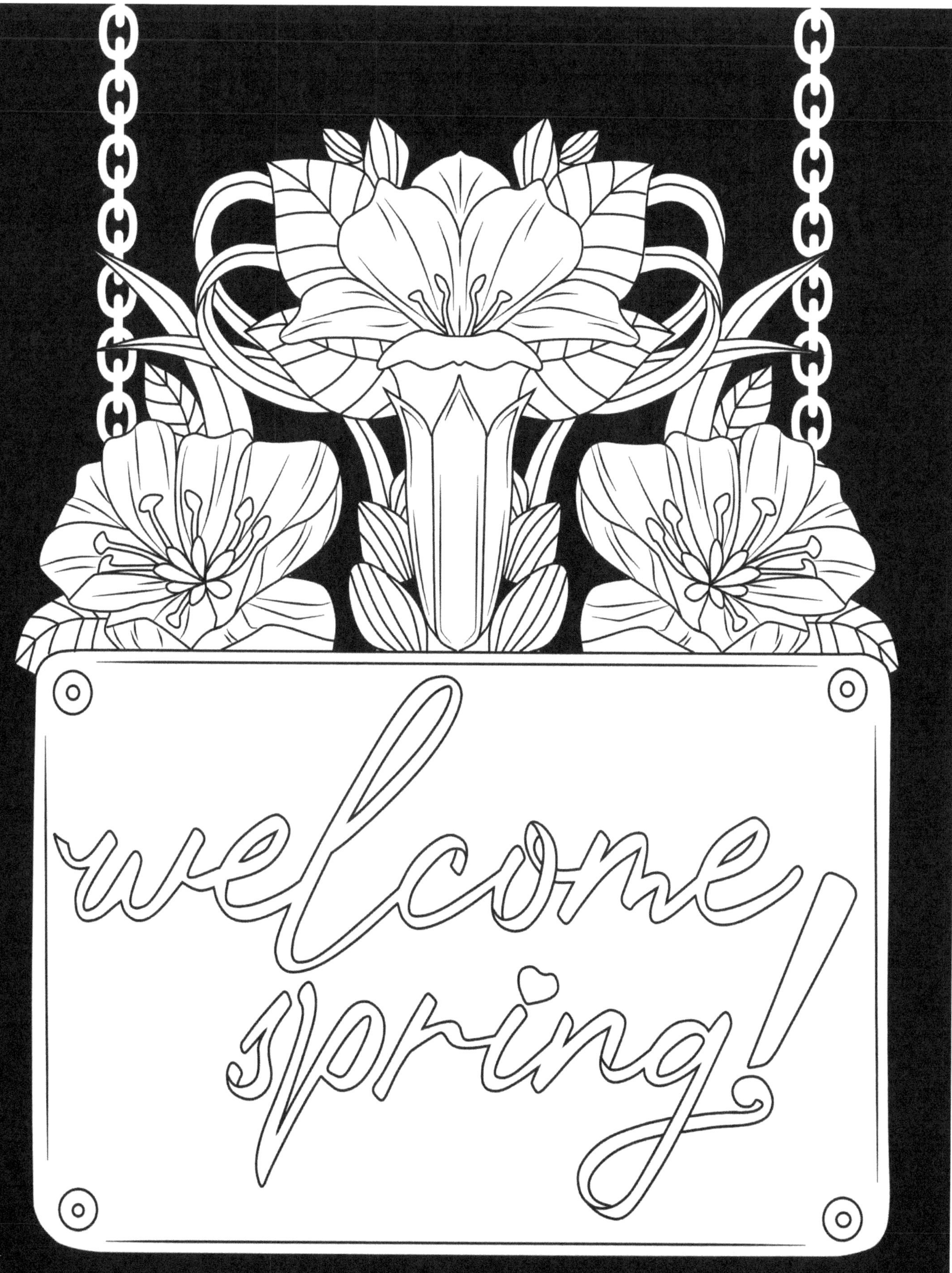
welcome
spring!

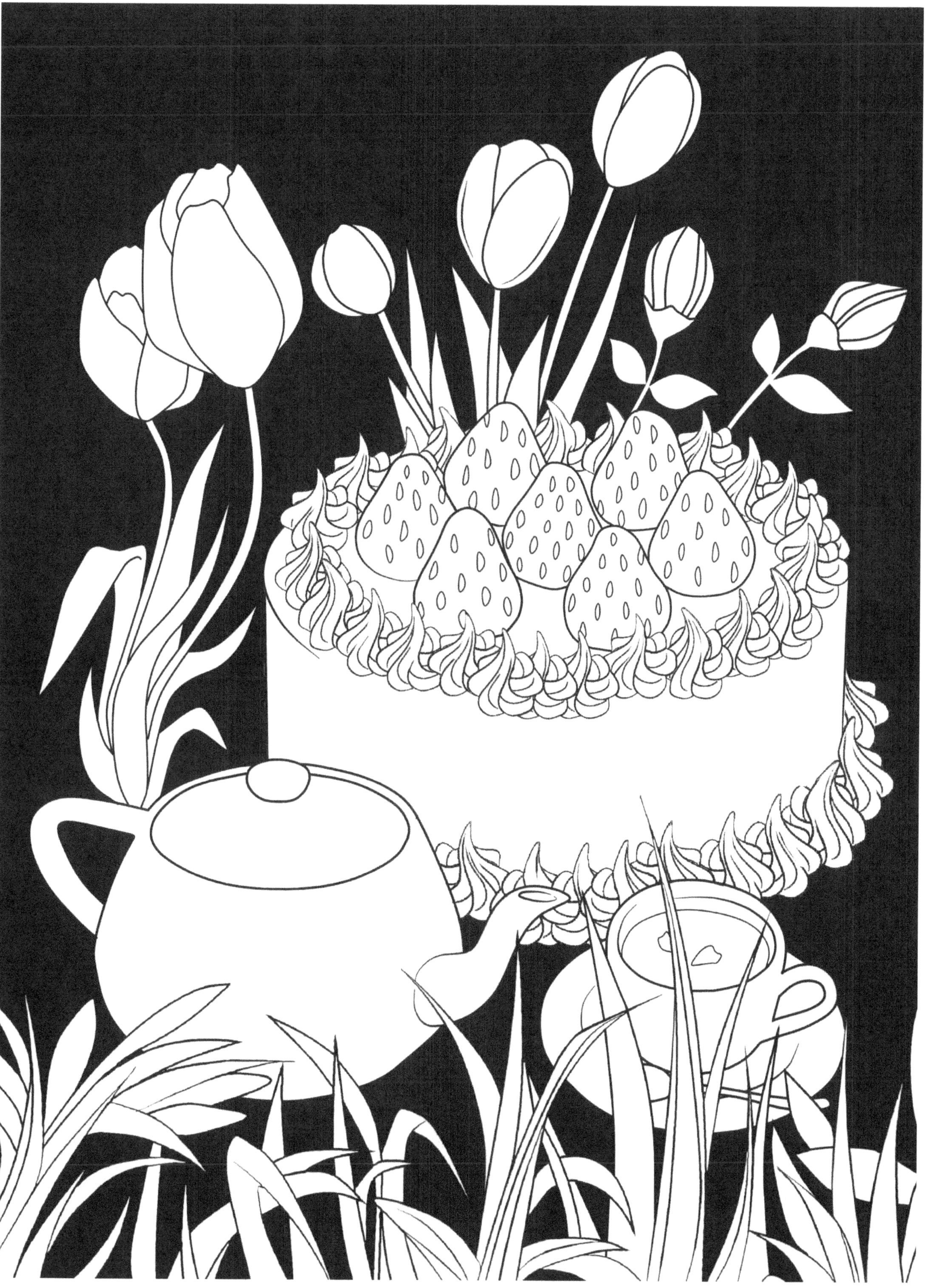

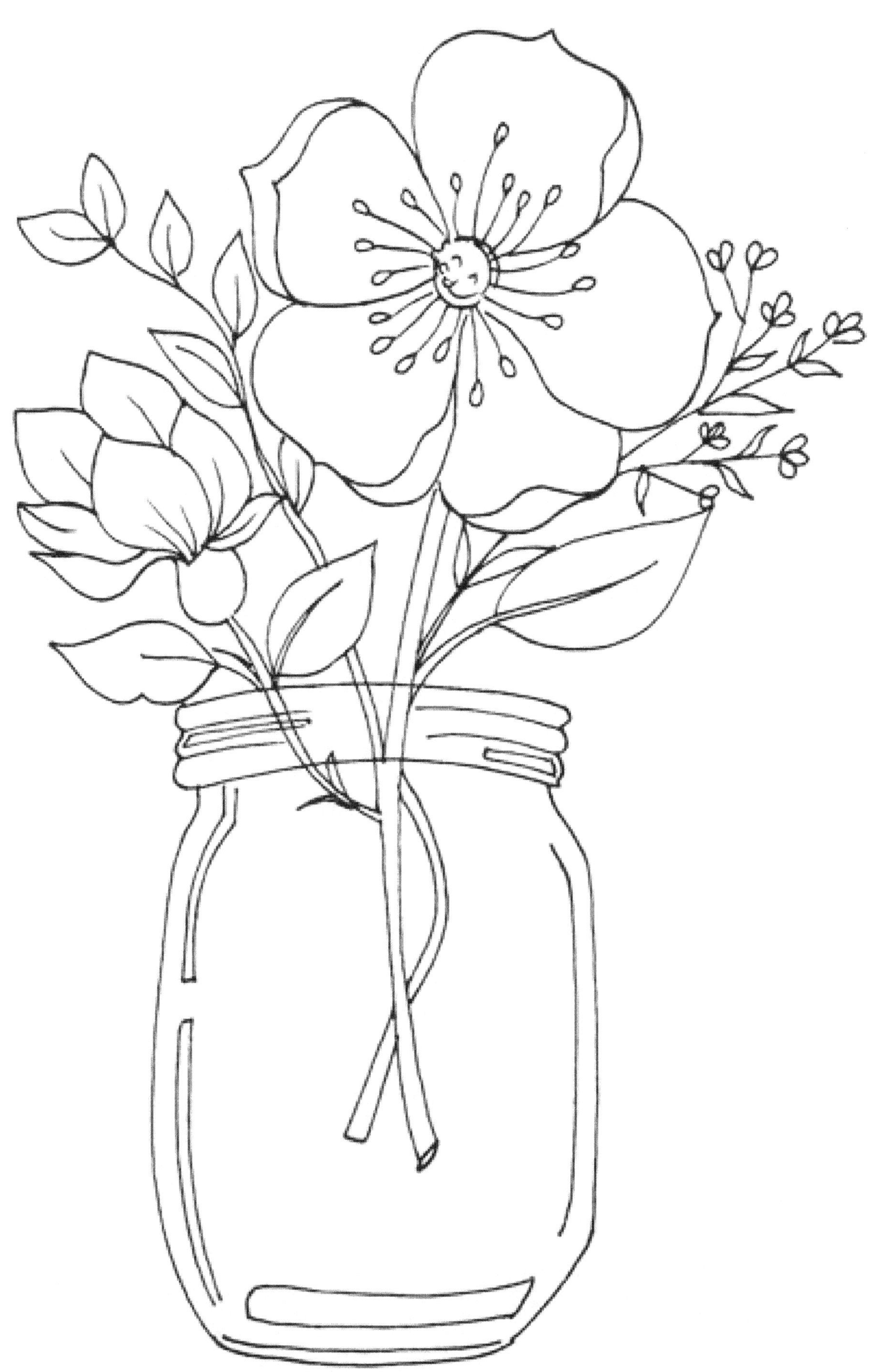

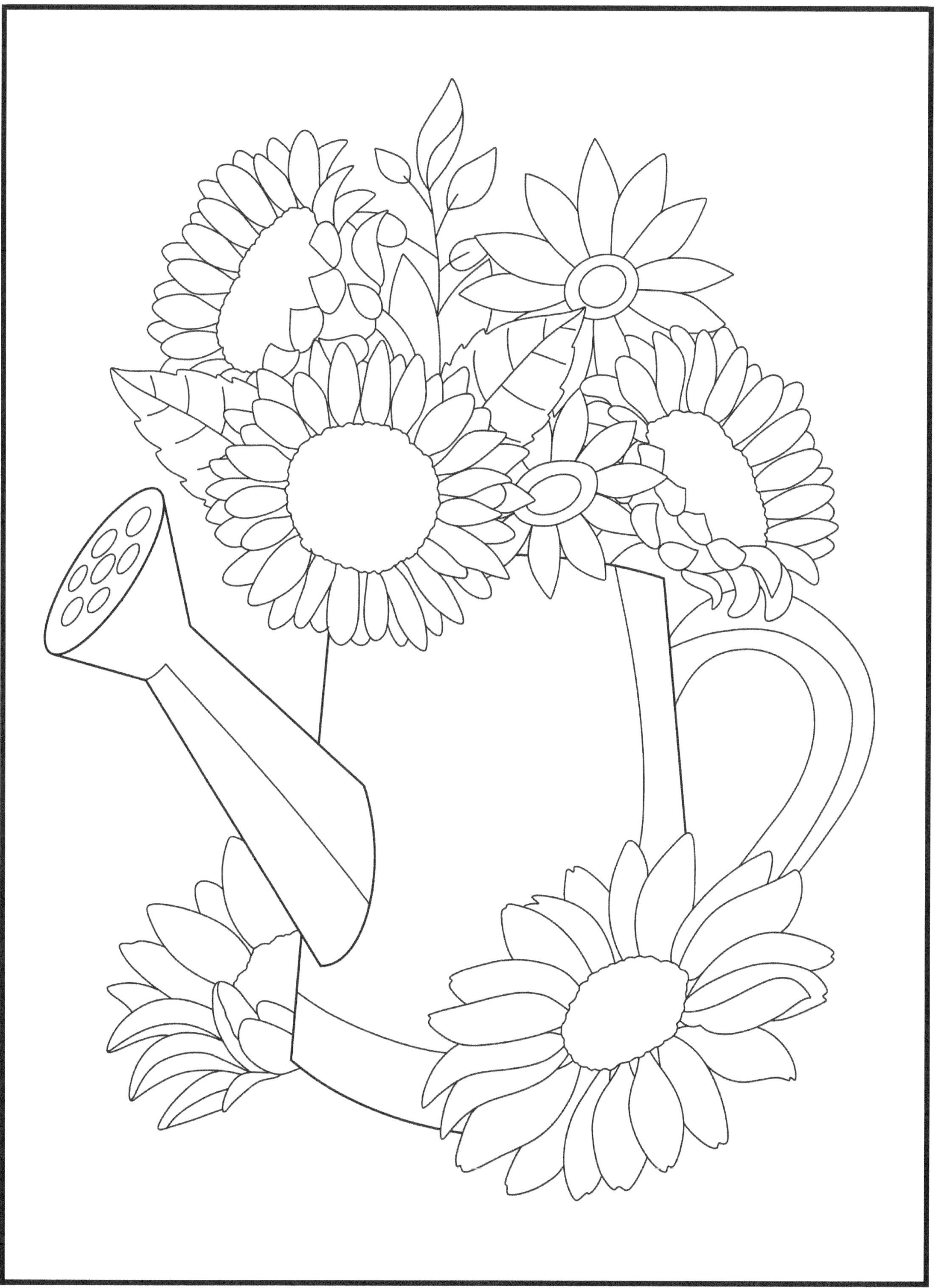

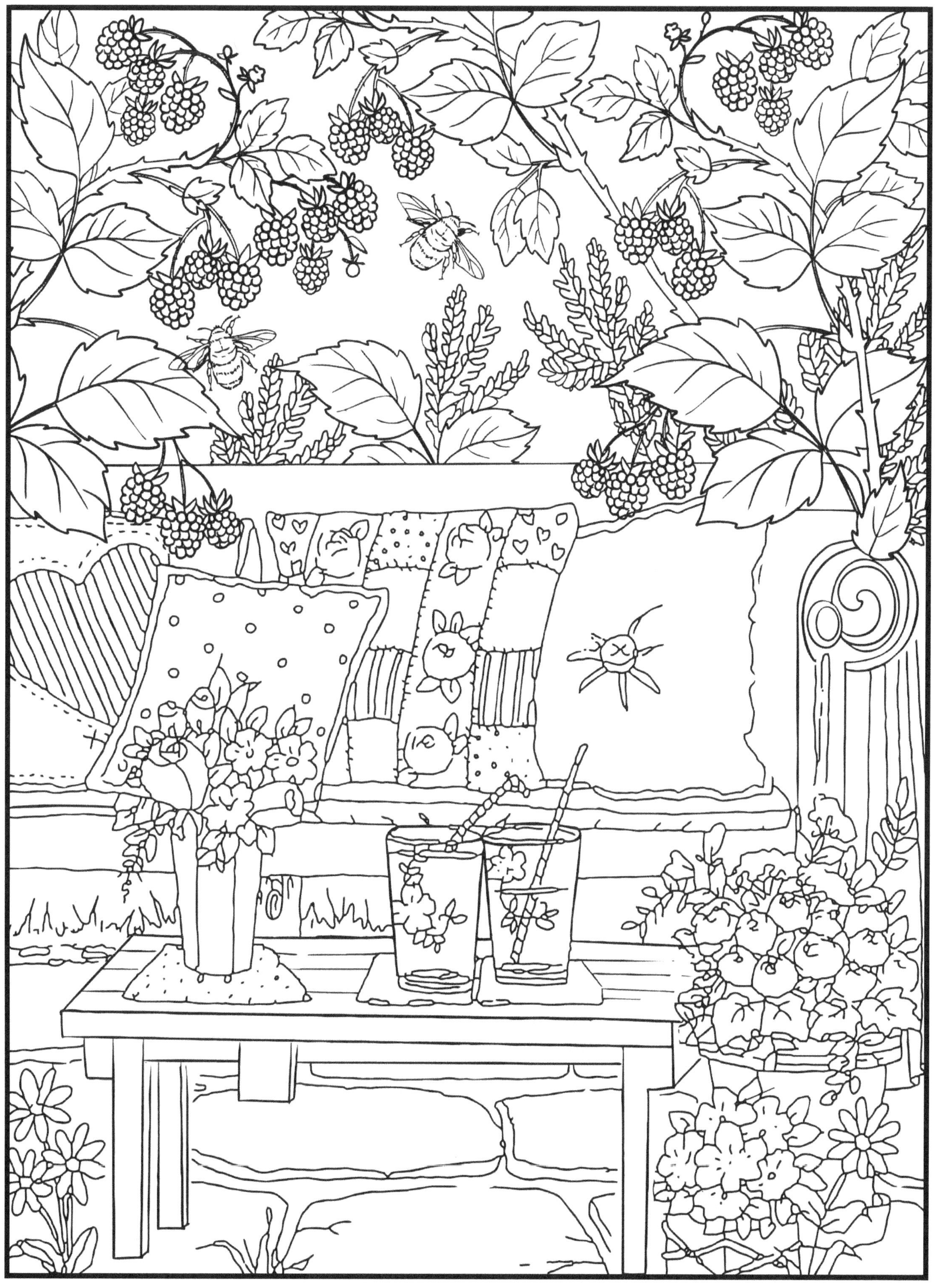

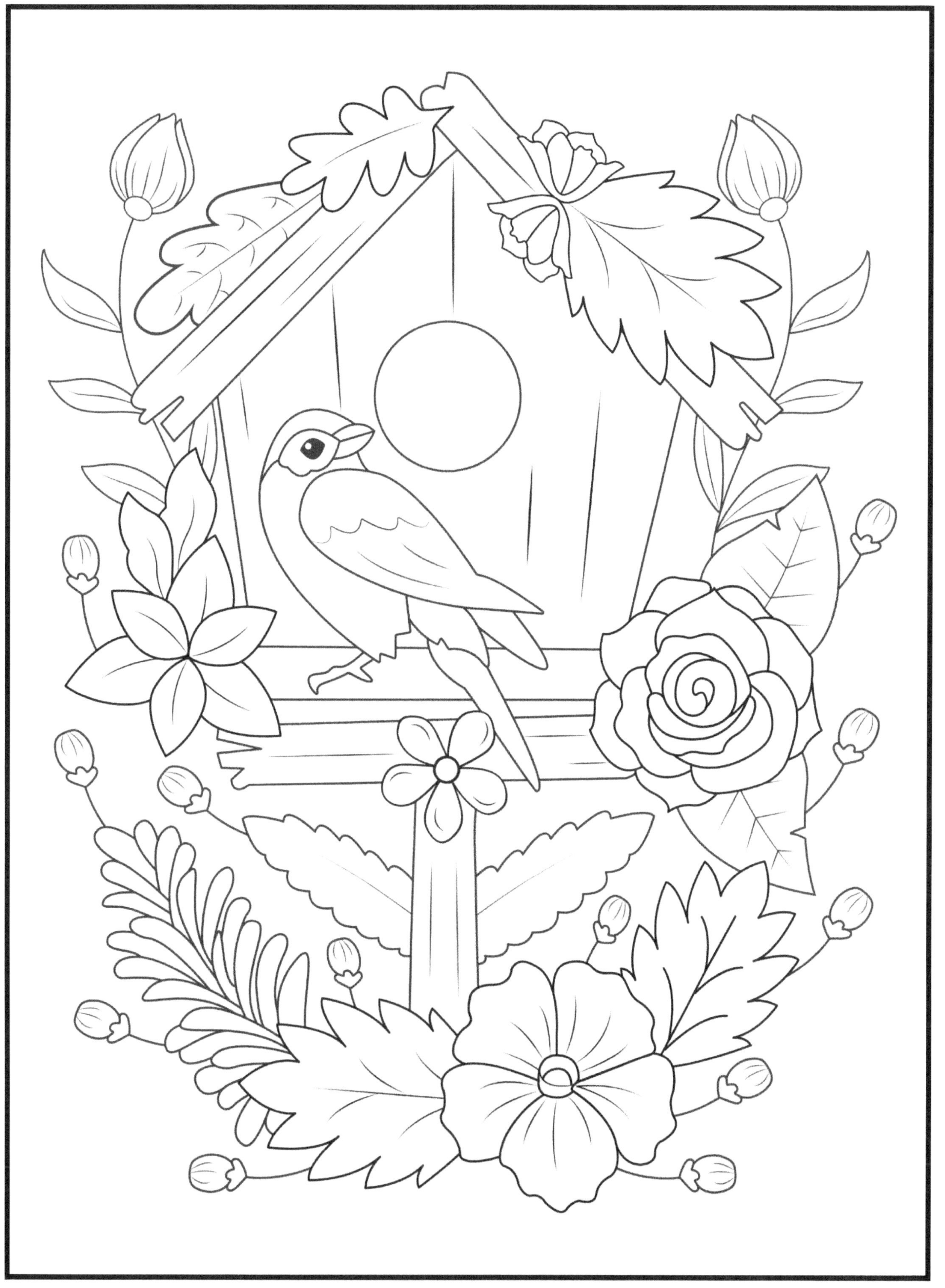

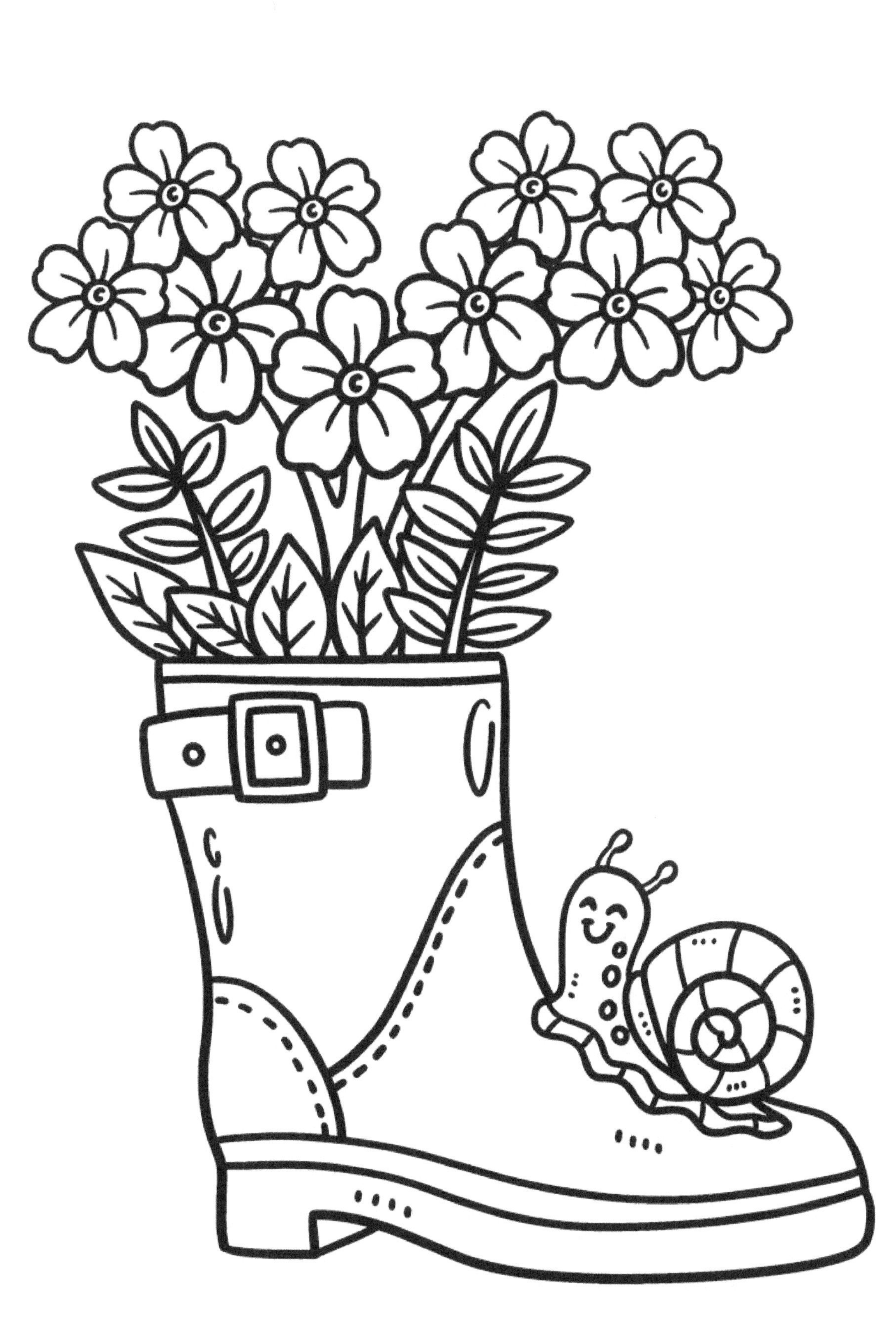

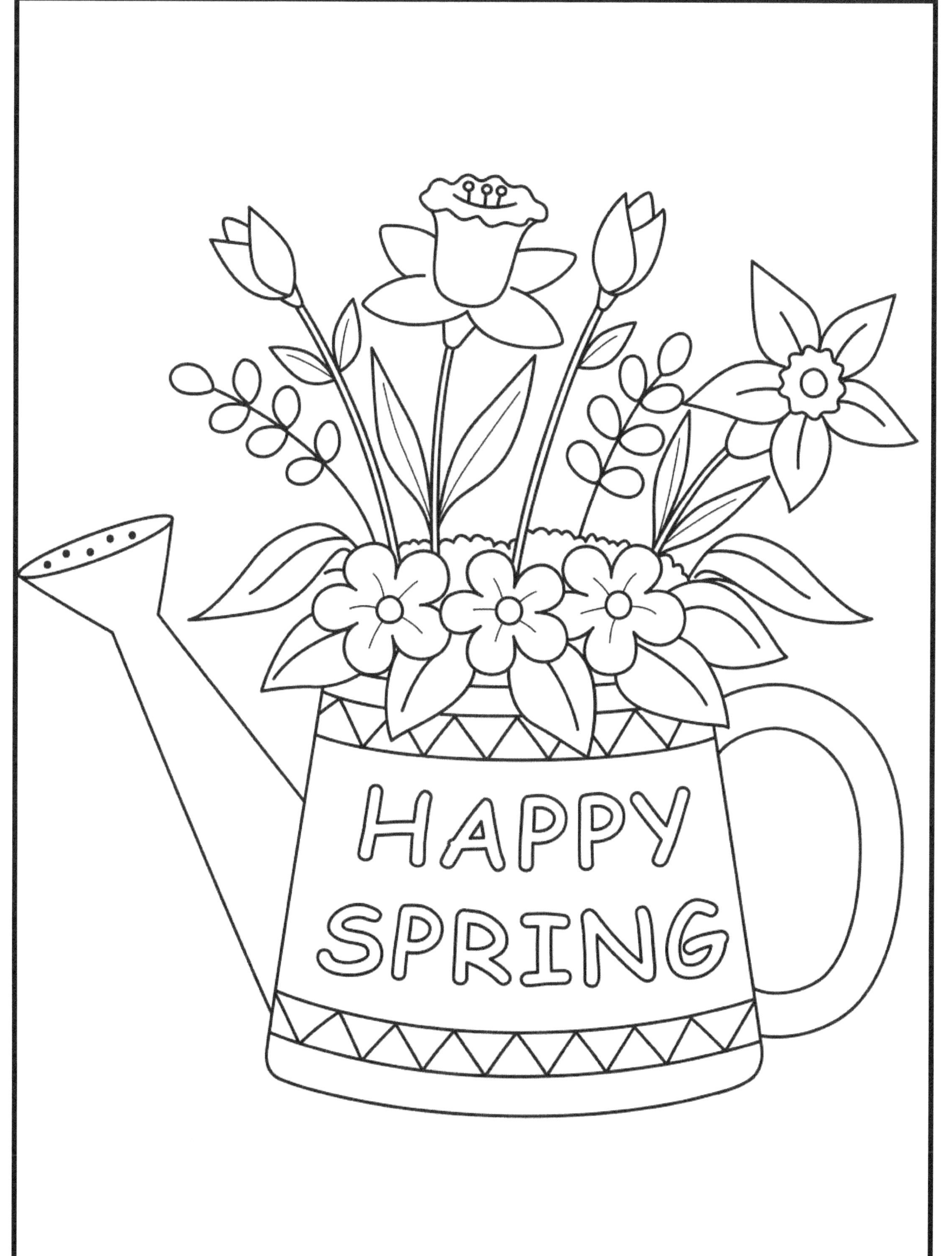
HAPPY
SPRING

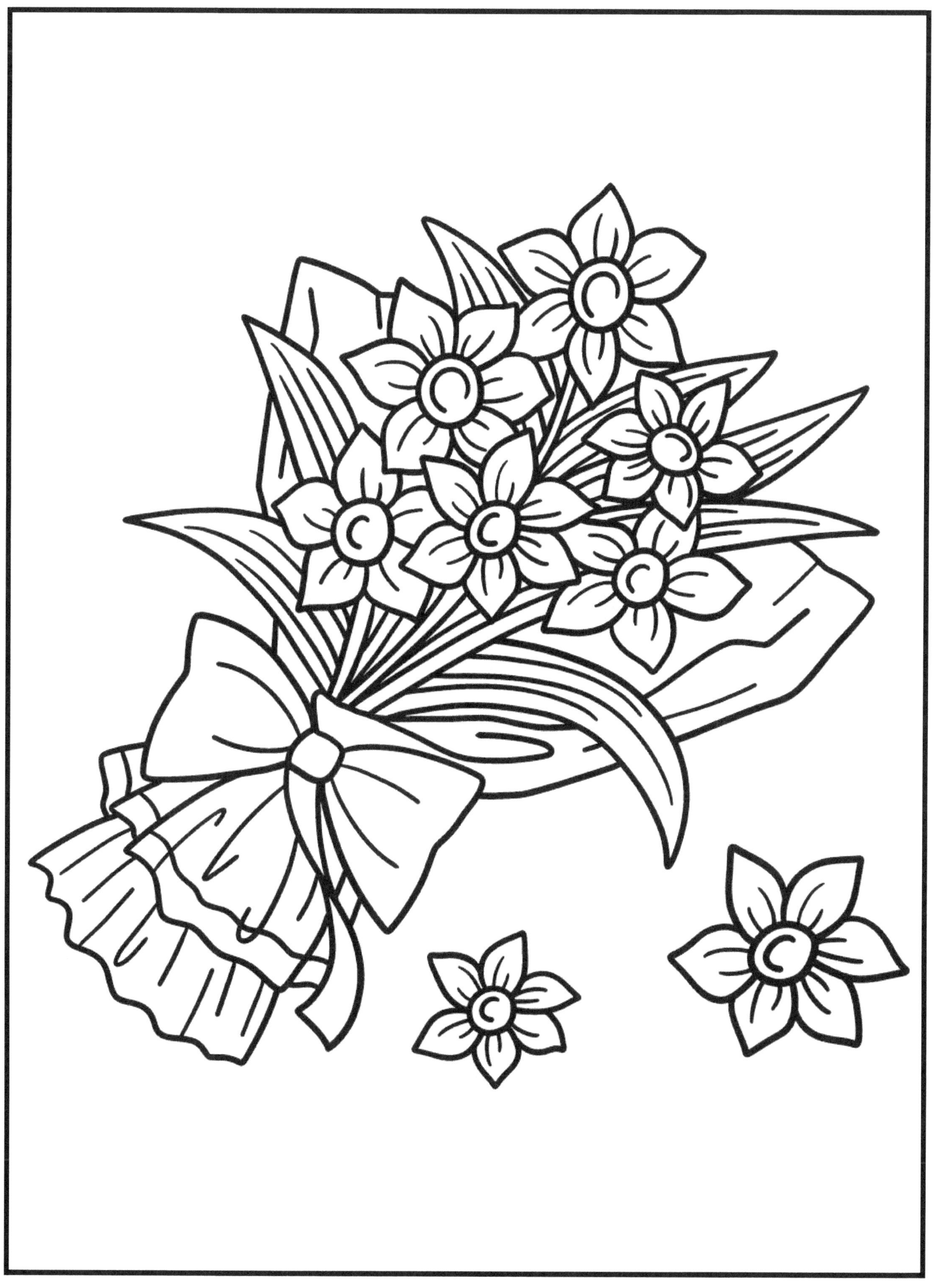

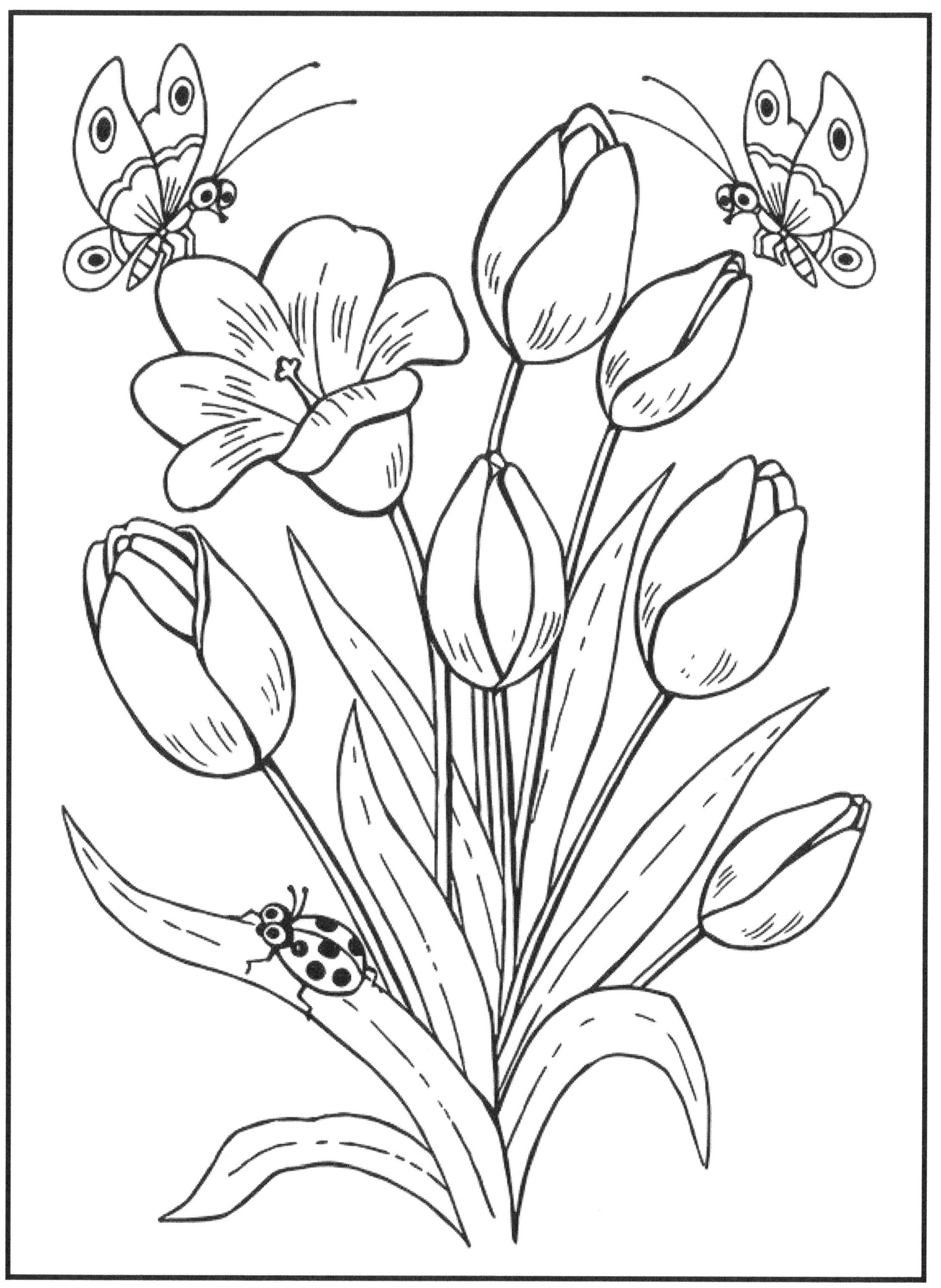

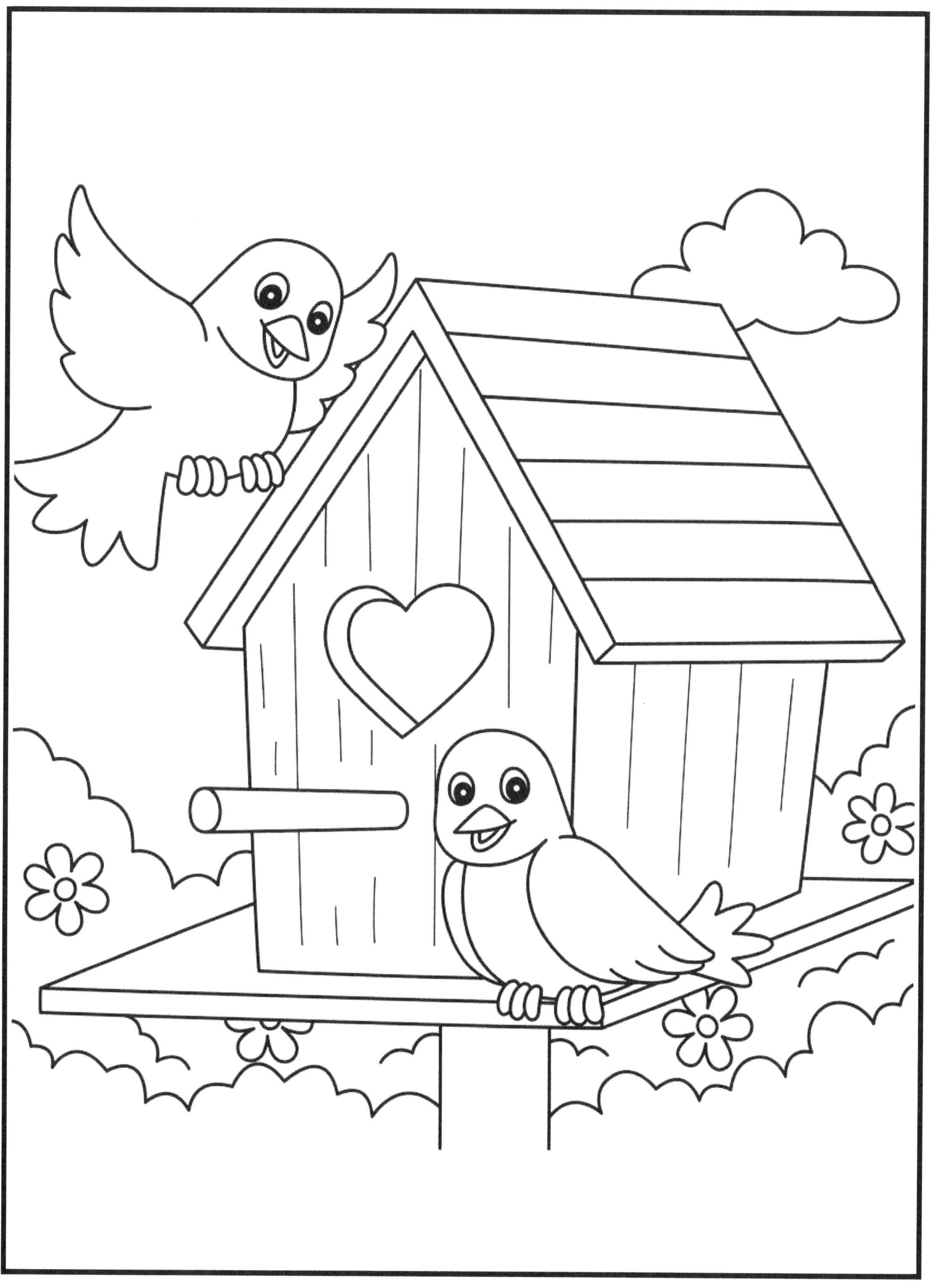

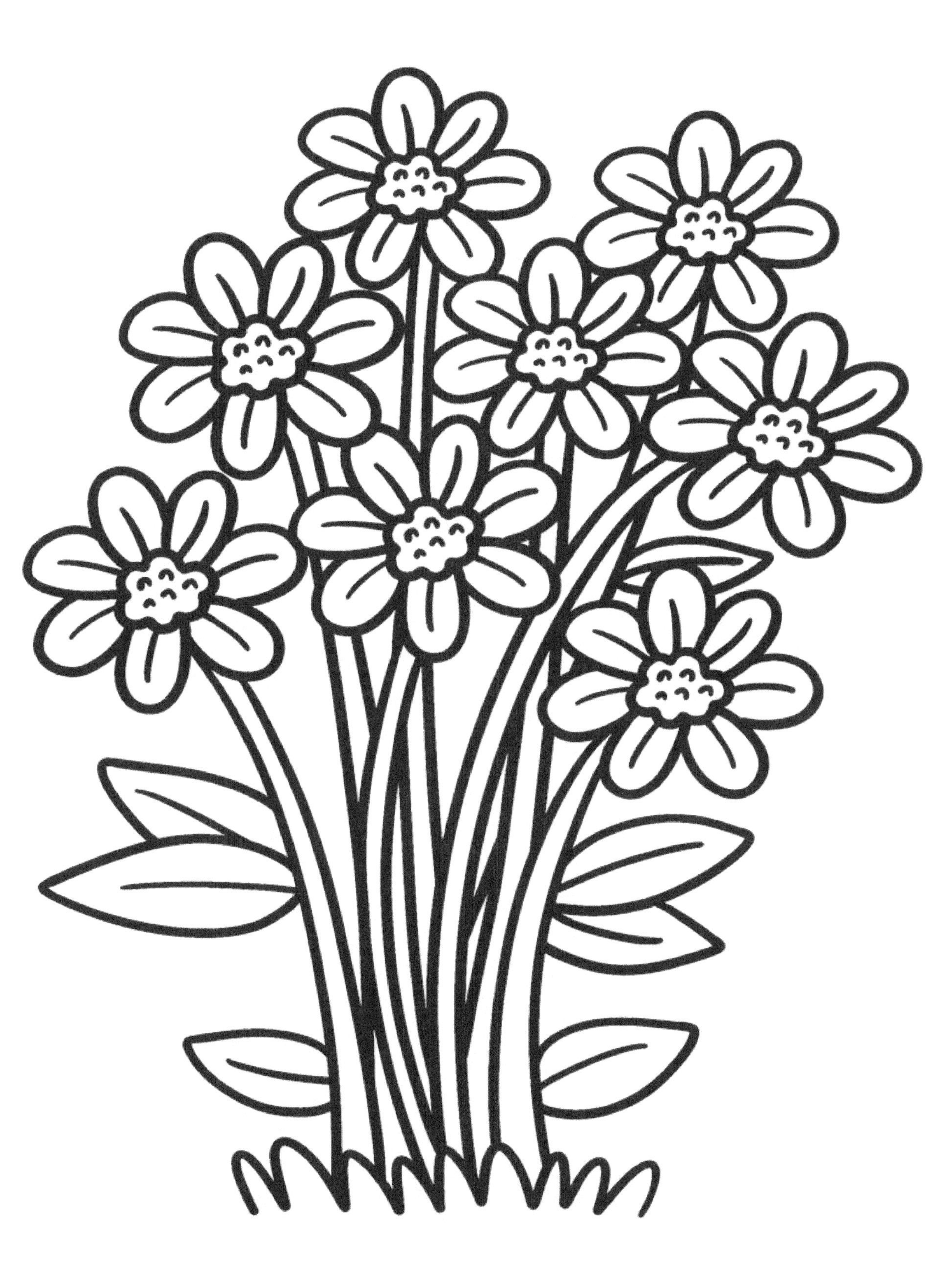

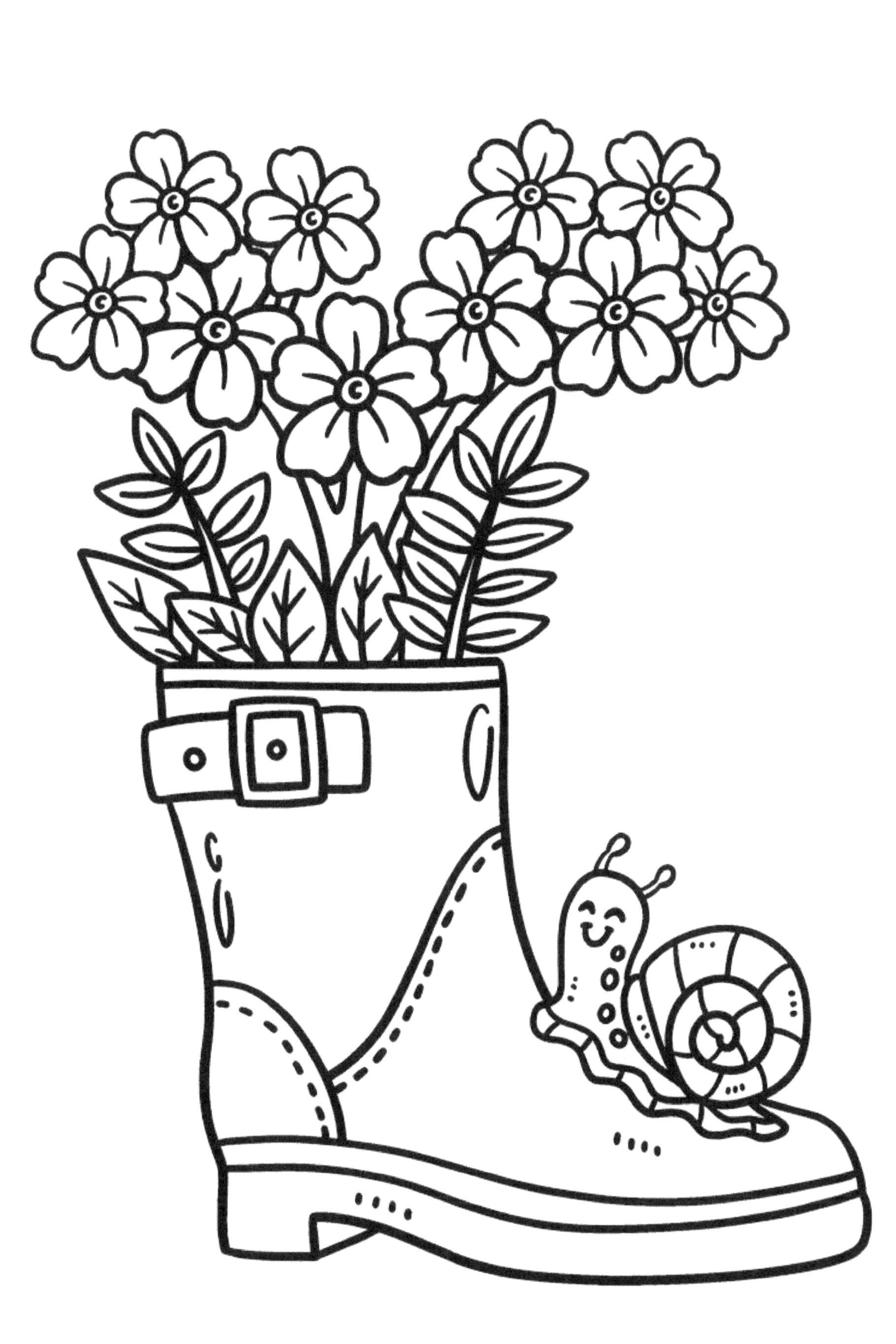

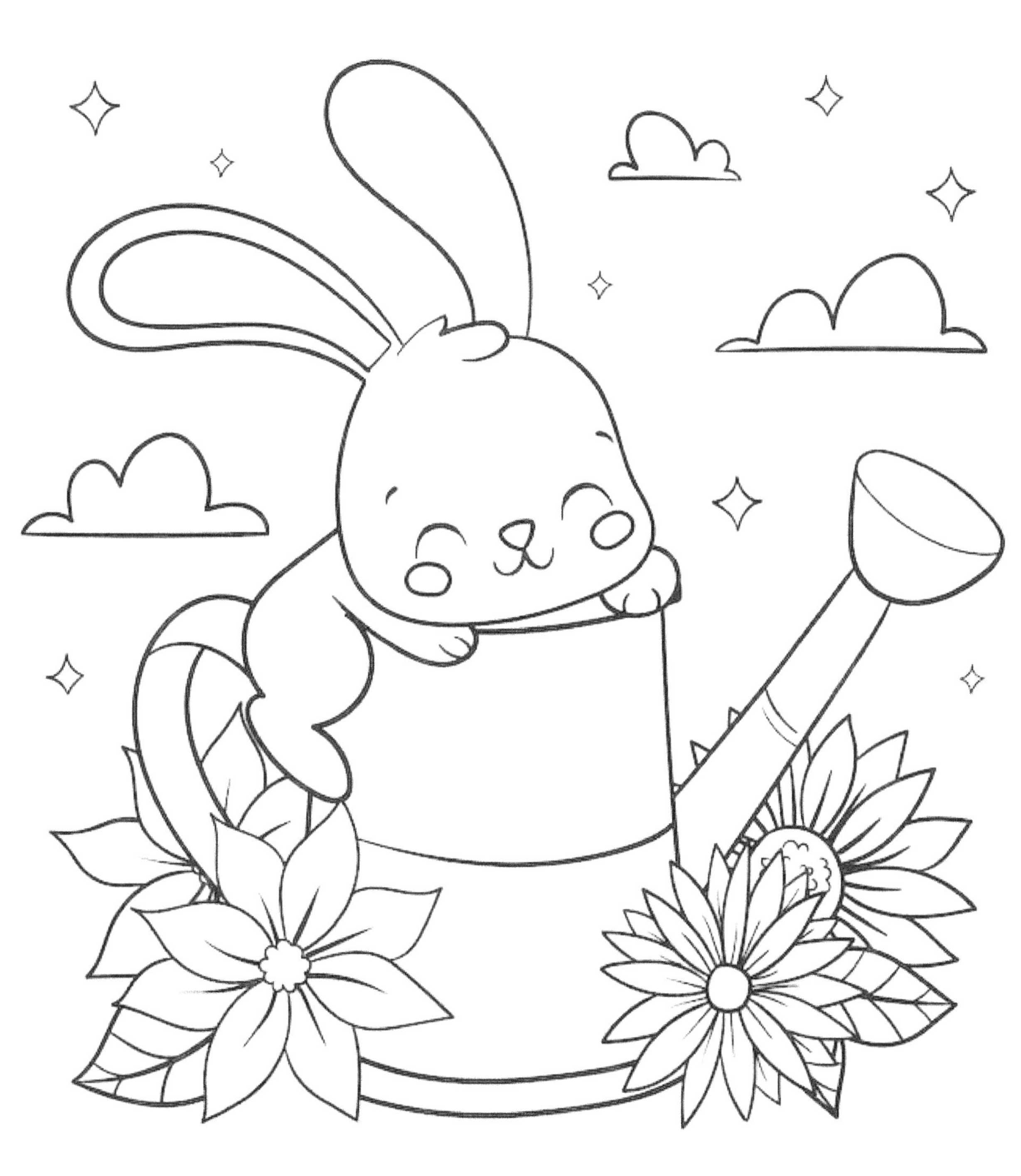

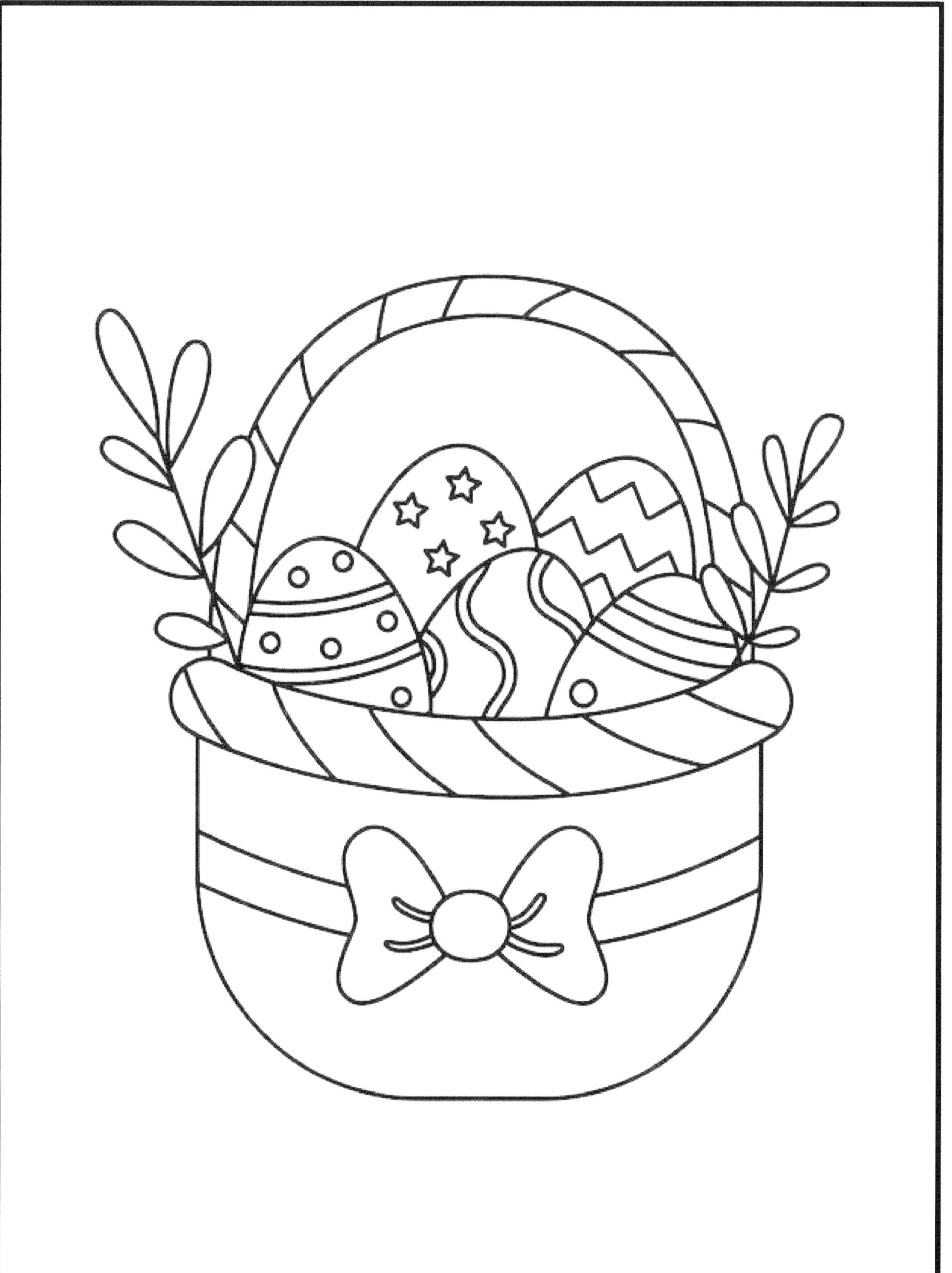

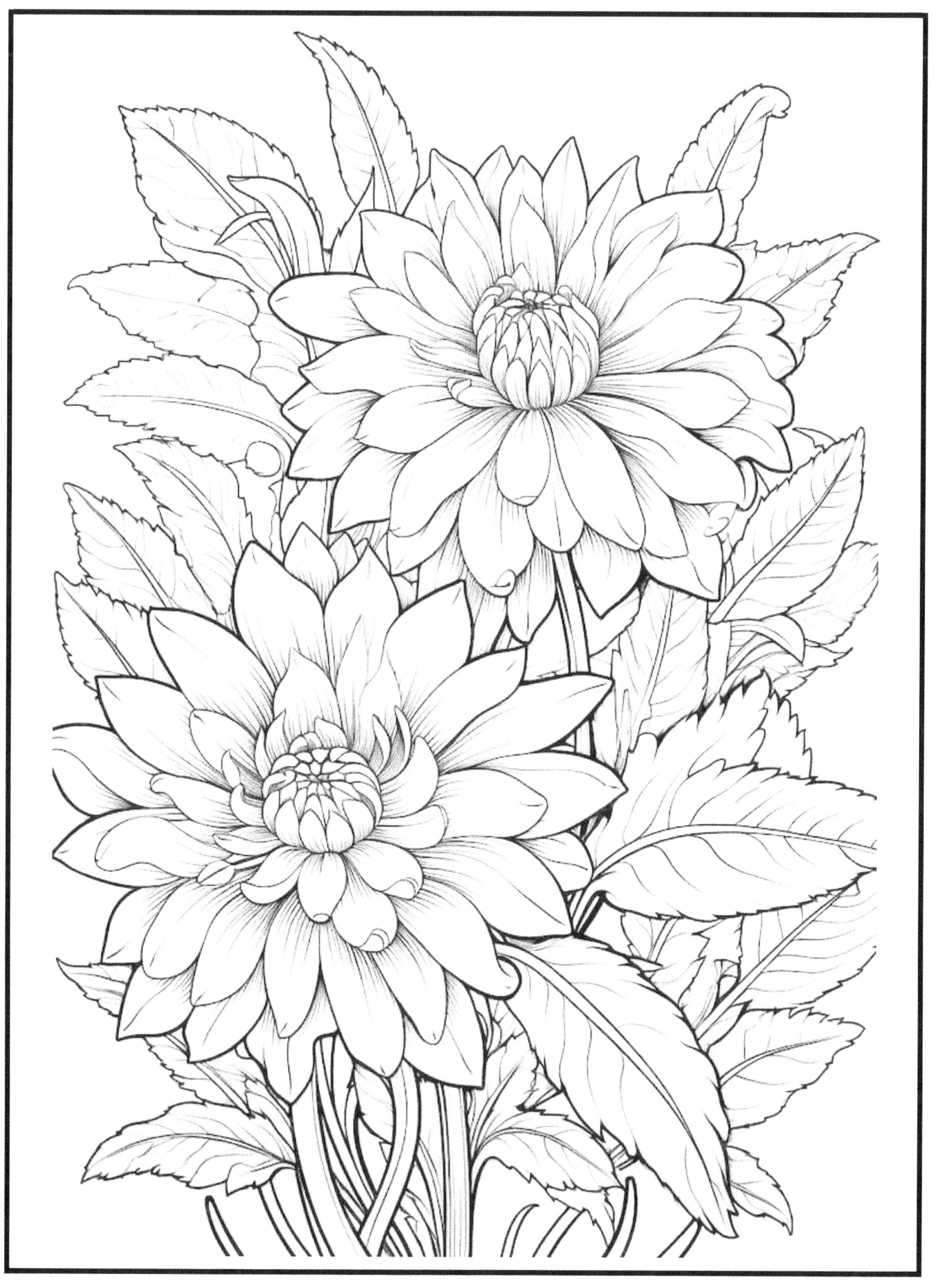

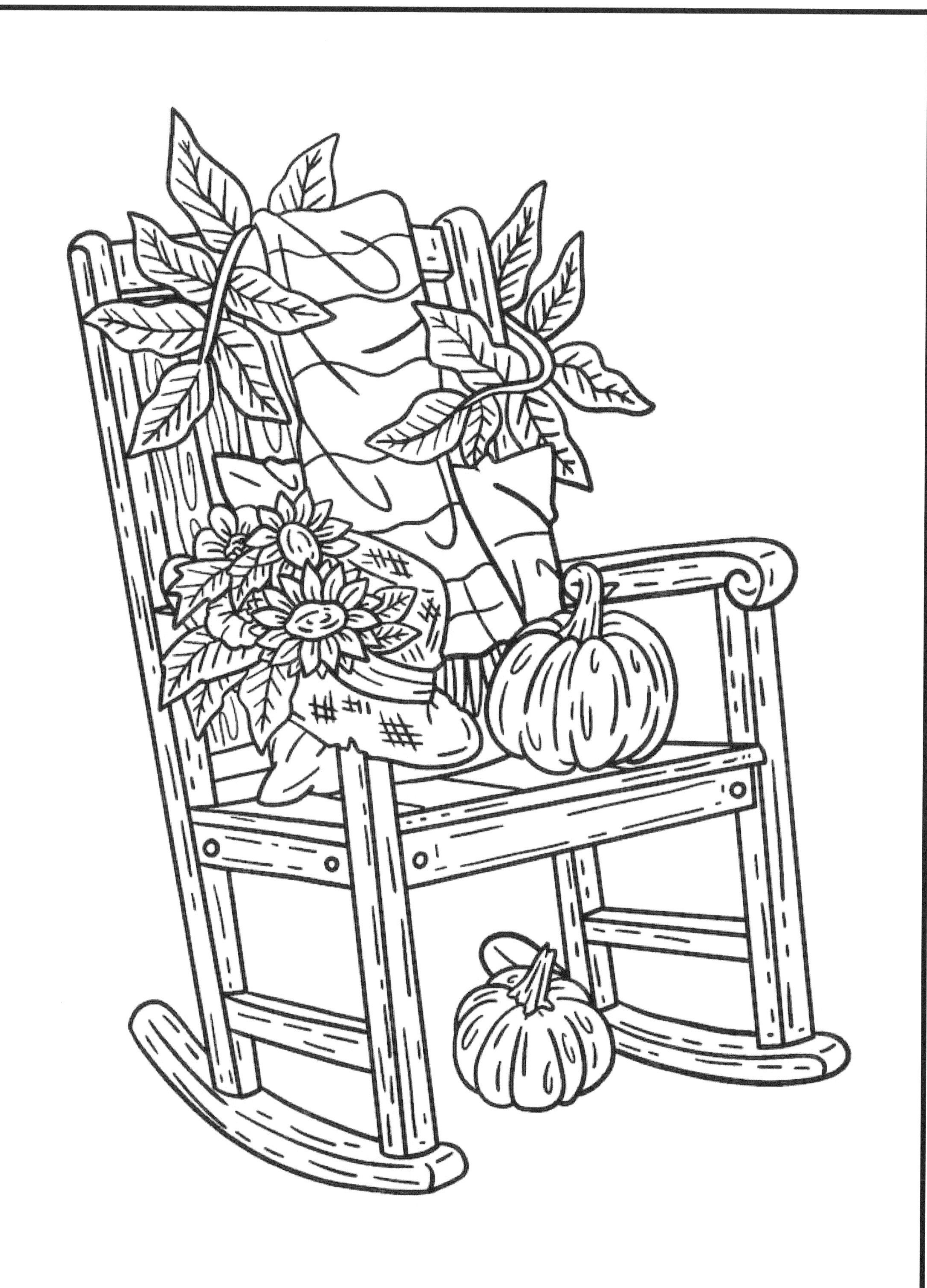

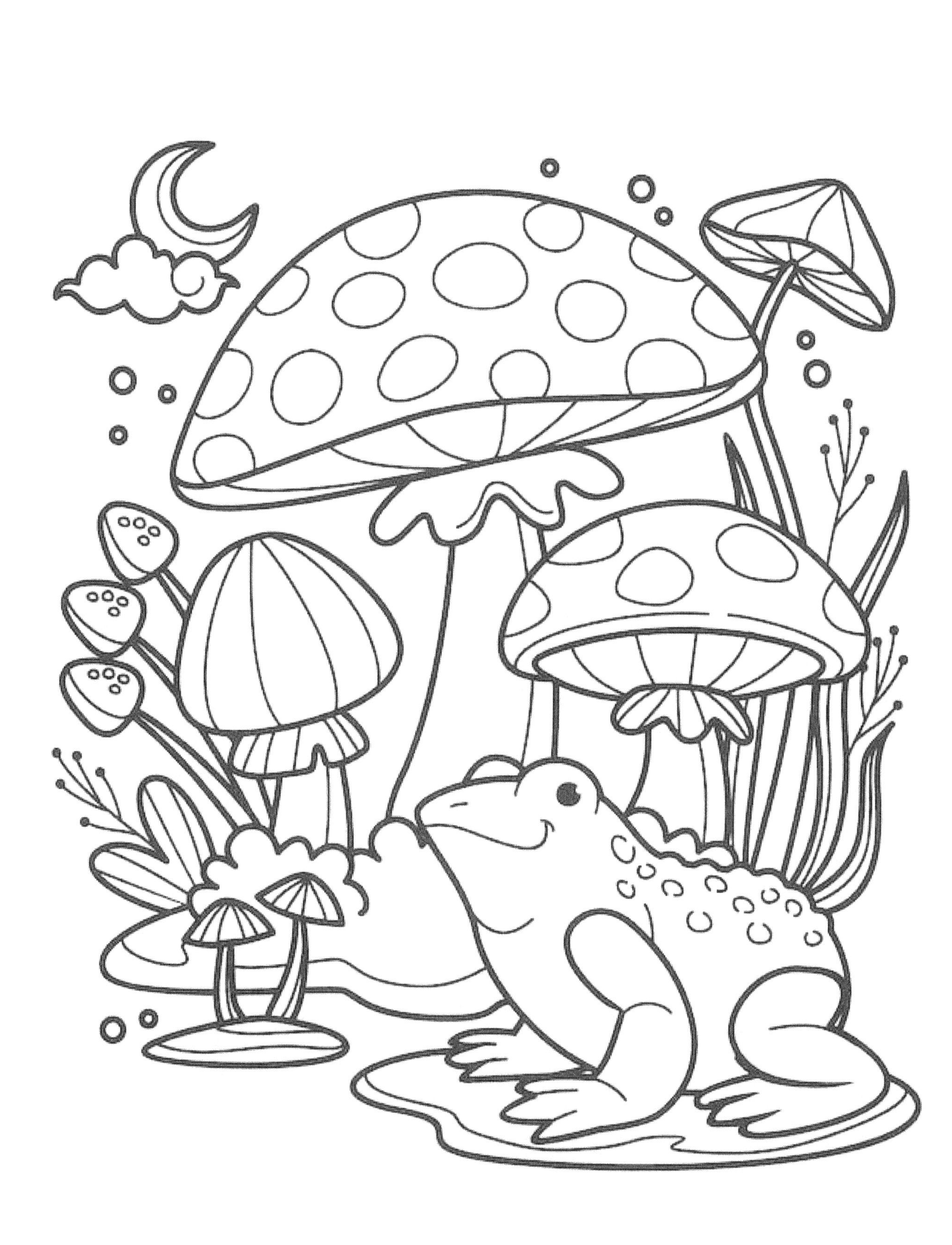

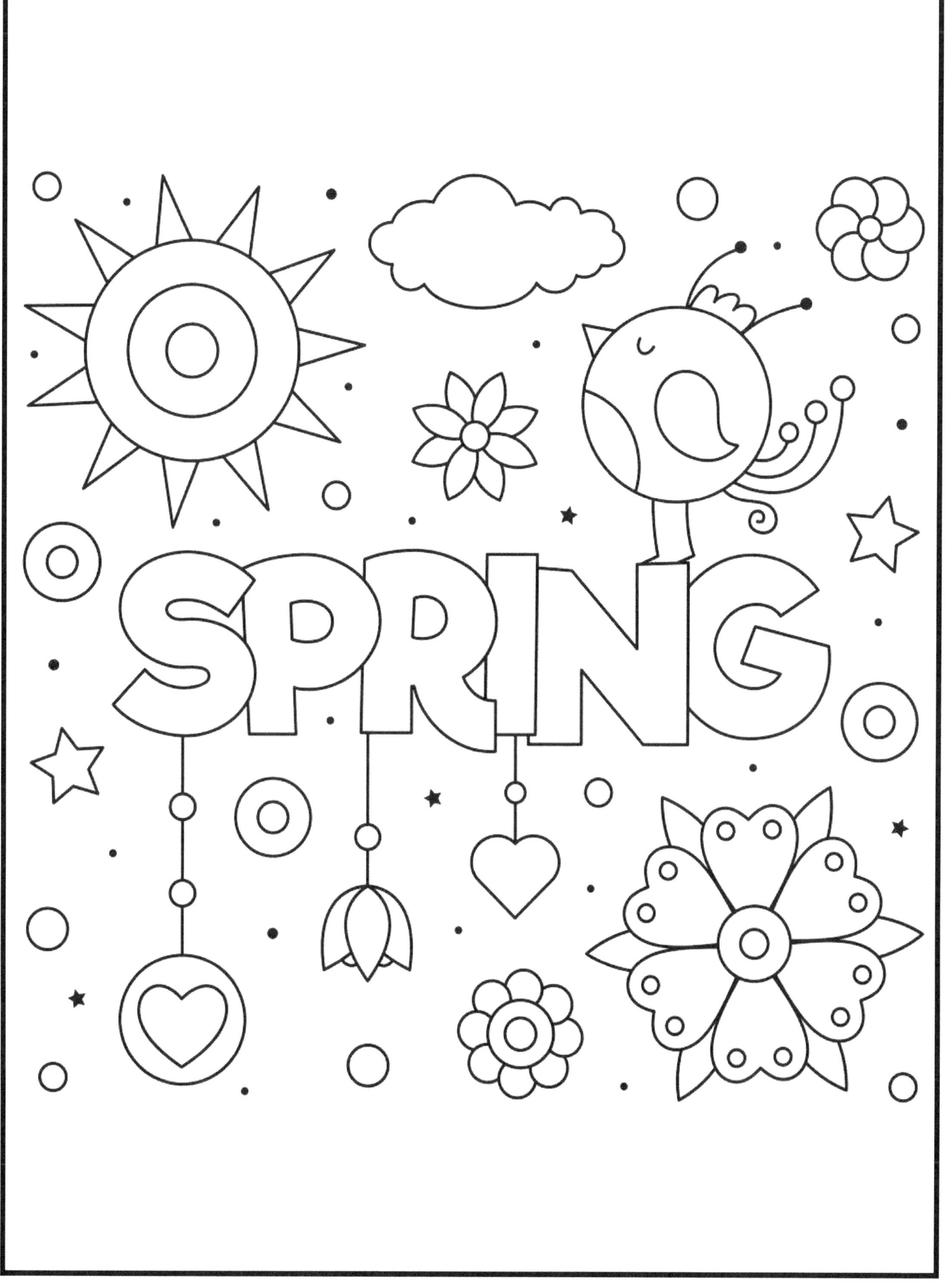
SPRING

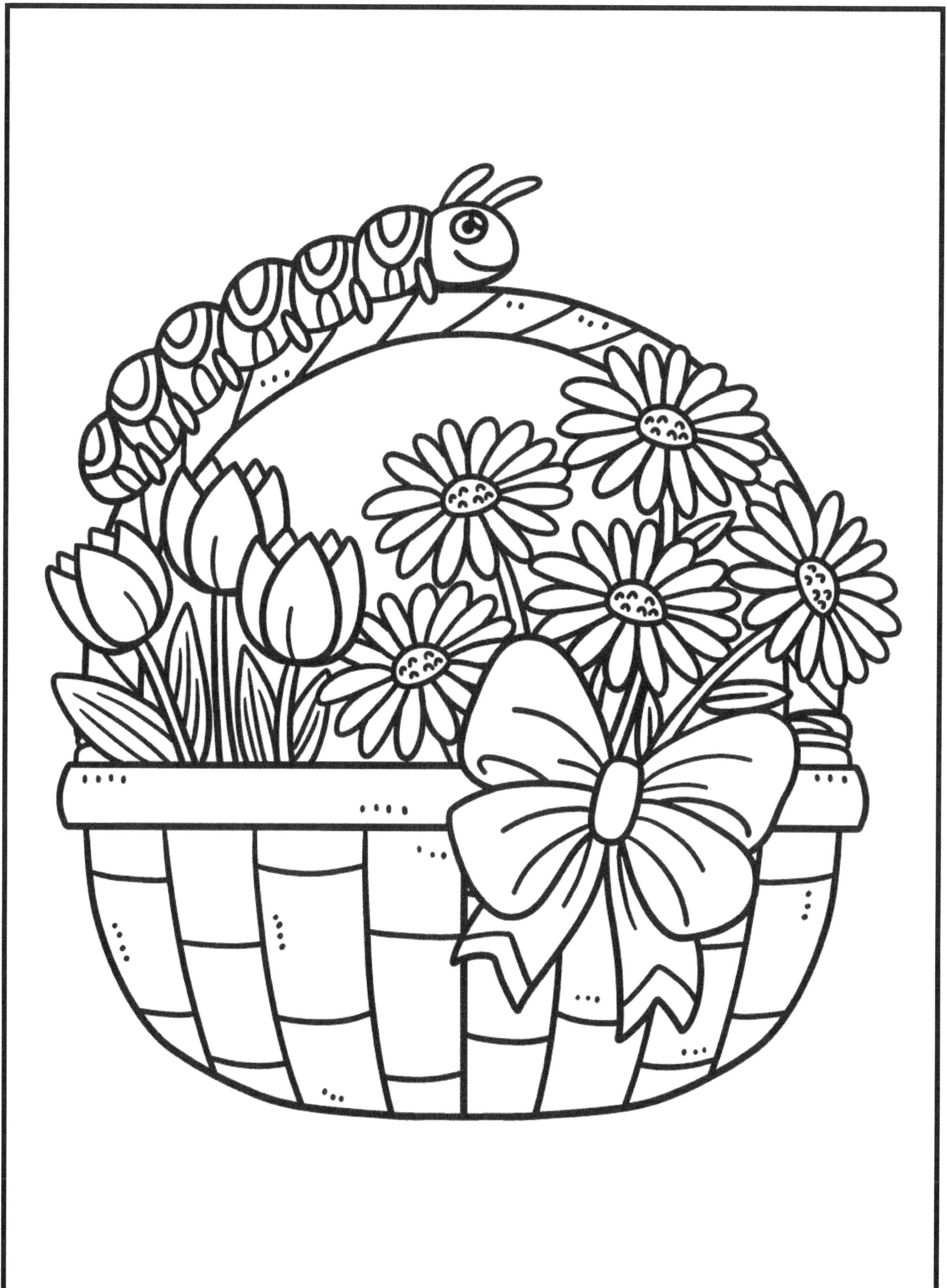

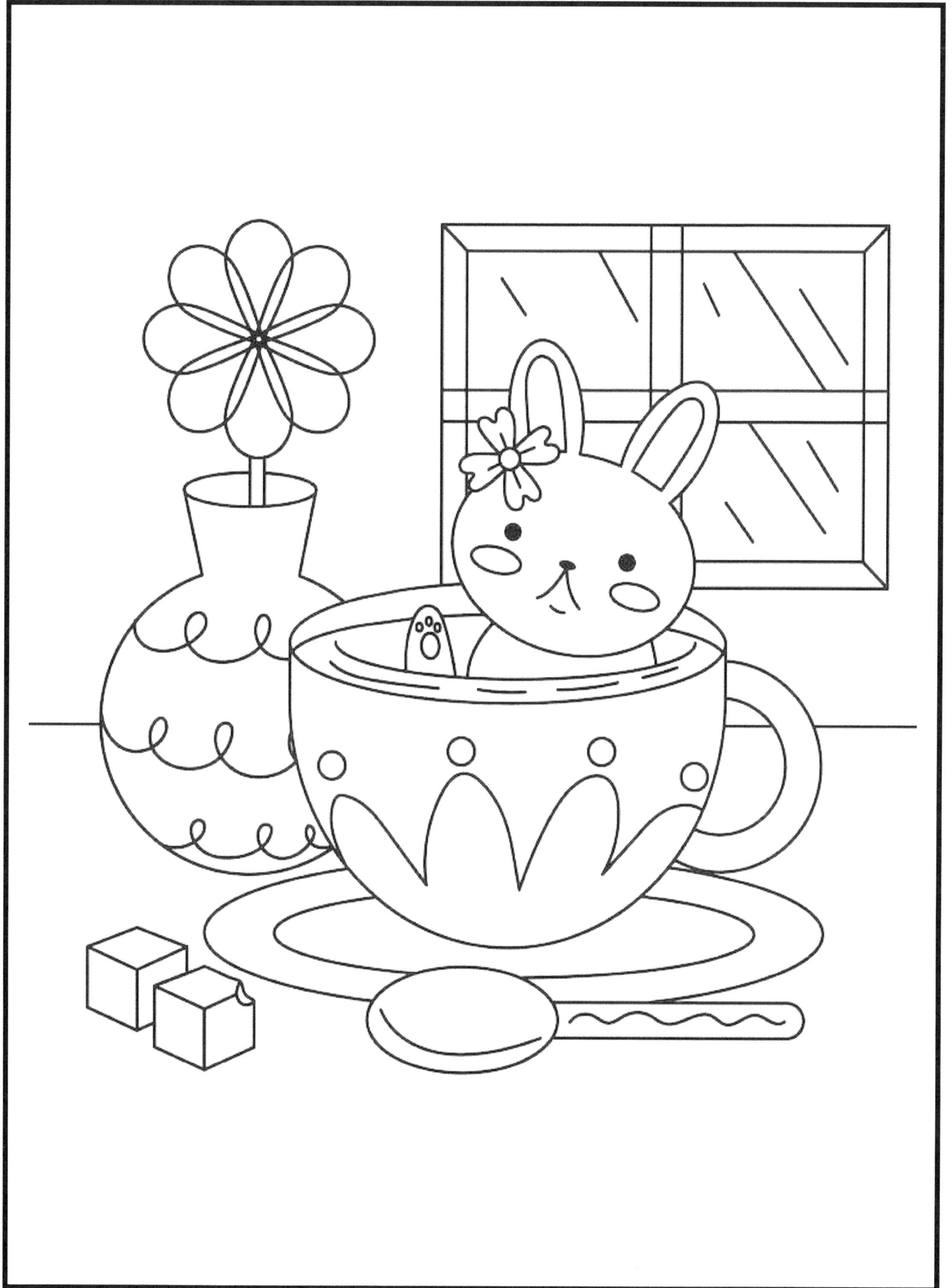